EXCEL

FOR

BEGINNERS

A Step By Step Guide To Mastering Microsoft
Excel And Unlocking The Full Potential Of
Spreadsheets For Beginners And Seniors,
With Tips, Tricks, And With Aid Of Pictures

By

DERRICK C. WAGNER

DISCLAIMER:

Table of Contents

INTRODUTION

Proficiency with Microsoft Excel, which has been around for quite some time, is highly sought after by employers in the data science and analytical industries. However, some people are just now beginning to use it. Starting out, whether for personal, academic, or professional reasons, might be a little daunting. Excel Basics is the focus of this blog. The best tool for manipulating data and making calculations is Microsoft Excel, so let's jump right in.

What Is Excel

Microsoft Excel (MS Excel) is an extremely versatile spreadsheet program. It has incredible uses in managing information and analyzing data. Excel is a spreadsheet program that lets you organize, modify, and deal with data in order to get, analyze, and change it. Spreadsheets allow you to conveniently organize and view information by allowing you to add text, photographs, videos, objects, and many more.

We may perform simple math calculations all the way up to more complex ones with the help of Excel, a Microsoft tool with built-in spreadsheets. We can open numerous spreadsheets at once in Excel.

HOW TO START WORKING WITH A NEW EXCEL SHEET

Go to the start menu of your system and search for excel.

After you have located the app, you can open it

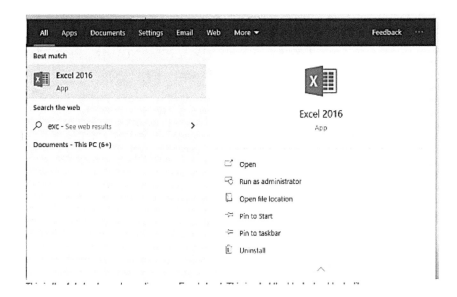

This is the first step towards your excel sheet. This is what black sheet looks like

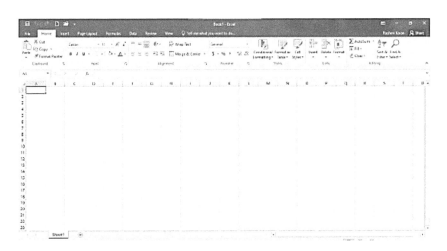

Add/ create/ delete/ tabs

- In the very bottom left corner of your freshly opened Excel spreadsheet, you'll see the reference to Sheet 1. Several tasks are at your disposal, as detailed below:
- Integrate a spreadsheet: To add a new sheet, find your most recent one and click the plus sign next to it.
- Sort assignments: Move the sheet to a different location in the spreadsheet by holding the tab.
- Pick out a spreadsheet: Press twice on the tab for the sheet and enter the new name. Sheet 1, Sheet 2, etc., will be the default names.
- Draw a tab on a spreadsheet: In order to apply a new tab color, simply right-click on the sheet tab and then click on the "Tab Color" option.
- Keep a spreadsheet safe: Add a password and choose your settings under Protect Sheet when you right-click the sheet tab.
- To copy or move a spreadsheet, right-click on the sheet tab and choose Copy or Move. After that, you can duplicate the page for each example, transfer it to a different workbook, or move it to a different location in the current workbook.
- To remove a spreadsheet, select the sheet tab in the toolbar, then click Delete. In the

subsequent pop-up box, you'll be asked to confirm this action.

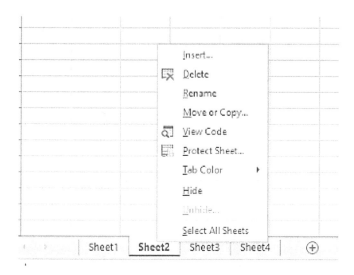

Excel ribbon

The ribbon is an important part of any Excel worksheet, therefore let's go on to it now. Word, PowerPoint, and other Microsoft Office apps have a ribbon interface that is very similar to this one. All of the buttons that will be used inside the tabs are held on the ribbon. Modifying the ribbon allows you to add or delete buttons and tabs. On the other hand, the tabs below should appear automatically.

On the main interface's ribbon, you'll see a set of menus and submenus. Through this, we will be able to access the majority of the program's integrated features. Actually, there are going to be a lot of features and functions here, so let's have a look at the ribbon's main characteristics.

The file: Workbooks can be made, opened, saved, printed, and shared.

Paste, align, style, numbers, cells, and editing are all under the "Home" menu.

Media: Add media such as tables, charts, images, links, etc.

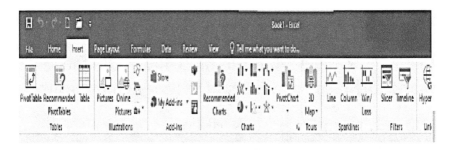

Layout of Pages: Modify the background color,

Formula: Run the formula audit by selecting a library function and a formula.

Data: organize, sort, analyze, manage, utilize data tools, etc.

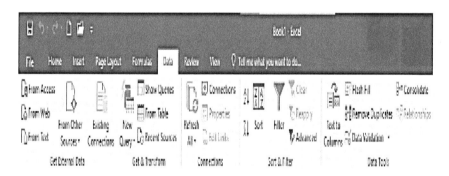

Examine: Make use of resources for grammar, spelling, thesaurus, feedback, etc.

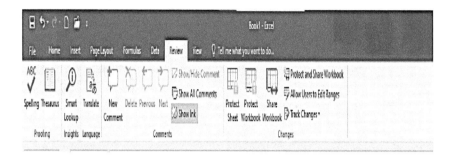

Change the view of the workbook, the items to show, the magnification level, and the number of windows you can work with.

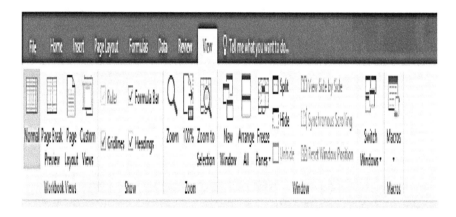

Rows and column in excel

Excel allows users to create and manage several linked spreadsheets. You can use columns and rows in any spreadsheet. A cell defines the connection between columns and rows.

Excel sheets are structured horizontally with respect to their rows. On the right side of the Excel page, you can see them arranged numerically from top to bottom.

	A
1	
2	
3	
4	
5	
6	
7	
8	
9	
10	

At the very top of each Excel sheet are columns that, when filled out, provide a vertical hierarchy to the data.

The intersection of the rows and columns is called a cell. Cell A2 is marked in a rectangle box in the illustration below, indicating that the data is in Column A and Row 2.

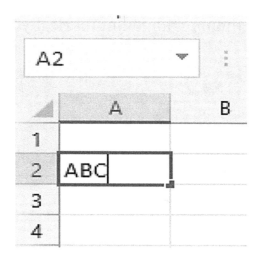

Quick access toolbar

You can customize the Quick Access Toolbar to have a set of commands that are separate from the ribbon. Its position in the Excel window is at the very top left. And it's crucial since it lets you swiftly save your file and undo or redo an activity.

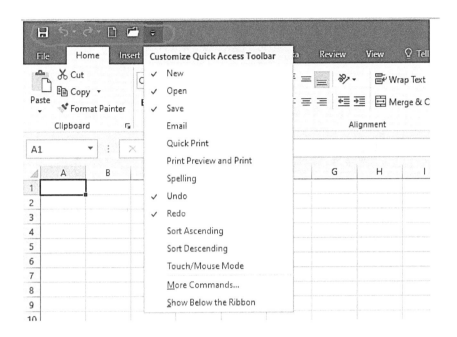

You can customize the Quick Access Toolbar and keep the options you want or use frequently.

Saving the sheet

Go to File. This interface will appear.

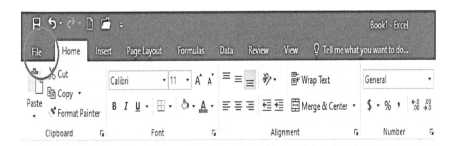

CHAPTER ONE

IMPORTANCE OF MICROSOFT EXCEL

1. Data Analysis and Management: Excel enables experts to efficiently handle enormous volumes of data. Excel is the preferred tool for data manipulation and analytics, from financial analysis to customer information organization.

2. Time-saving: By mastering complex Excel formulae and functions, staff may automate time-consuming operations and free up more time for strategic decision-making.

3. Enhanced Productivity: People can increase productivity and improve workflow efficiency by streamlining different processes with Excel's many capabilities.

4. Improved Decision Making: Robust data analysis in Excel yields insightful information that helps with well-informed decision-making and promotes the expansion and success of businesses.

5. Project management: Better planning, tracking, and reporting are made possible by

Excel's adaptable project management templates and features, which guarantee successful project execution.

6. Financial Modeling: Excel is a valuable tool for finance professionals and analysts as it is commonly utilized for financial modeling and forecasting.

7. Presentation and Visualization: Professionals can show complex data in an aesthetically pleasing and easily comprehensible way by utilizing Excel's graphing and charting tools.

8. Data Validation and Error Checking: The data validation tools in Excel contribute to the preservation of data integrity and accuracy by reducing errors.

9. Cross-Functional Applicability: Excel proficiency is useful for workers in a variety of fields, as it is applicable in departments like finance, marketing, human resources, and operations.

10. Employability: Learning Excel will greatly improve your employability and career prospects. It is frequently a requirement for many job situations.

HOW TO IMPROVE YOUR MICROSOFT EXCEL SKILL

1. Online Tutorials and Resources: To learn both fundamental and sophisticated Excel operations, make use of free online tutorials, blogs, and video platforms.
2. Practice Regularly: The more you practice, the better you become. To improve your abilities, make example projects or work with actual data.
3. Master Formulas and Functions: To efficiently manipulate data, concentrate on mastering the fundamental formulas (such as VLOOKUP, SUMIFS, and IF) and functions.
4. Examine Add-ins for Excel: Learn how to enhance Excel's features and automate processes by utilizing add-ins.
5. Attend seminars and Webinars: To learn from professionals and obtain fresh perspectives, take part in Excel-focused seminars or webinars.
6. Join Excel-related forums and groups to ask questions, exchange ideas, and pick up tips from more seasoned users.
7. Use Templates: To save time and learn how different functions are implemented

in real-world circumstances, make use of pre-built Excel templates.

8. Online Excel Challenges: Take part in online Excel competitions or challenges to put your skills to the test and pick up tips from other competitors.

9. Enroll in Comprehensive Courses on Advanced Excel Features, Data Analysis, and Visualization Techniques: Make an investment in thorough courses covering these topics.

10. Acquire reputable Excel certificates to prove your abilities and establish your credibility in the employment market.

The quickest route to better Excel proficiency is through consistent learning and targeted practice. Make a systematic learning plan that includes practice on a regular basis, goal-setting that is doable, and progress monitoring. Engage in practical projects and push yourself to take on challenging assignments requiring in-depth understanding of Excel. Get input from mentors or peers to pinpoint areas that need work and use the finest Excel usage practices.

DATA ENTRY AND EDITING IN EXCEL

Entering data:

A worksheet allows you to enter text, numbers, and formulas. Anything other than numbers or formulae is considered text. When doing computations, numbers are utilized as values. Using formulas is like doing math.

Filling out a cell with data:

- Pick out the cell.
- Begin inputting the information.
- An insertion point appears as you type, and the text you are entering is displayed in both the active cell and the Formula bar.

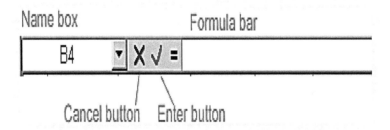

- There are two buttons on the Formula bar: Enter and Cancel.
- After pressing the Enter key

ends the entry and turns off the Formula bar buttons.

Text can be entered in Formula bar or in cell

To delete data:

Choose the cell.

AND

Select the "Cancel" option. To remove an entry and disable the buttons on the Formula bar, click the Cancel button.

Instead, you can use the Escape key to delete a field.

OR, use the context menu that appears when you right-click and select Clear Contents.

OR

Press either Enter or Delete to choose the data.

Crucial aspect. The AutoComplete function in Excel remembers what you type in one column and can fill in blanks there. In cell A2, Excel will fill in the blank with GCFLearnFree.org if you entered G in cell A1, for instance. Press type or Tab to go to the next cell if GCF Global Learning is the text you wish to type. Just keep typing until you overwrite the AutoComplete feature if it's not what you want.

DATA EDITING

Data entered into a cell can require editing or changing. One of two approaches will do.

For the simple and fast approach:

To replace an existing entry with a new one, just click the cell and type.

Edit the lengthy original entry if it only needs a small change (in spelling, for example).

To edit the formula bar entry, click the cell.

An alternative is to double-click the cell. By doing so, you enable direct editing in the cell.

Click the Formula bar's Enter button or hit the Enter key on your keyboard. Click the "Enter" button to finish entering.

Text can be entered in Formula bar or in cell

	A	B	C	D
1		**First Name**	**Address**	**Phone**
2		Jay	123 Street	555-5555
3		Lisa	456 Street	555-1213
4		To	789 Street	555-6789
5				

Microsoft Excel - Book2

File Edit View Insert Format Tools Data Window

Arial   10   **B** *I* U

B4   X ✓ = To

When working in Excel, the active cell is the one that is currently selected. To select a range of cells, go to the first cell in the range. The mouse pointer will turn into a big cross. To select the last cell in the range, hold down the left mouse button and release it. The cells you selected will be shaded. To select all the cells in a column or row, click on the column or row heading. To select multiple columns or rows, click on one heading and drag to select the others.

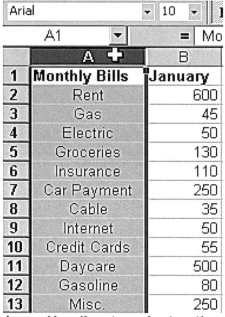

	A	B
1	**Monthly Bills**	**January**
2	Rent	600
3	Gas	45
4	Electric	50
5	Groceries	130
6	Insurance	110
7	Car Payment	250
8	Cable	35
9	Internet	50
10	Credit Cards	55
11	Daycare	500
12	Gasoline	80
13	Misc.	250

Click Column Heading to select entire column

A1 = Monthly Bills

	A	B	C	D
	Monthly Bills	**January**	**February**	**March**
2	Rent	600	600	600
3	Gas	45	60	55

Click on Row Heading to select entire row

To select the entire worksheet:

In order to choose the whole worksheet, click the gray rectangle on top left.

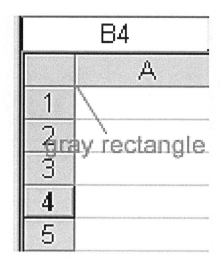

If you wish to choose multiple ranges of cells or columns that aren't adjacent to each other, you can do that by picking one range at a time while holding down the Control key. As an example, you might only be interested in columns A and C, and not B.

CHAPTER TWO

BASIC FUNCTIONS IN EXCEL

1. Formulas

An expression that manipulates values in one or more cells in Excel is called a formula. As an example, consider the formula =A1+A2+A3, which finds the total of the values in cells A1–A3.

2. Functions

Excel functions are formulas that have already been specified. While providing them names that are easy on the eyes, they do away with the tedious process of manually entering formulas. Consider the following expression: =SUM(A1:A3). The values of A1 through A3 are added together using the function.

FIVE TIME SAVING WAYS TO INSERT DATA INTO EXCEL

There are five standard methods for including elementary Excel formulas in data analysis. There are benefits to either approach. So that you can establish your chosen workflow earlier on, we will discuss those approaches before digging further into the key formulas.

1. Easy insert: entering a formula into the cell

Adding simple formulas to Excel is as easy as typing them into a cell or the formula bar. Typing an equal sign followed by the name of an Excel function is the standard starting point for the process.

Excel is quite smart; a function hint will appear as you start to type the name of the function (see below). Your choice will be taken from this list. But wait! After you've made your choice, don't hit Enter. Instead, you may just hit Tab, and Excel will fill in the name of the function for you.

2. Making Use of the Formulas Tab's Insert Function Option

Utilizing the Insert Function dialogue box in Excel is all that's required if you desire complete command over the insertion of your function. This may be accomplished by navigating to the Formulas tab and then selecting the first menu that says Insert Function. To finish your financial analysis, you may find all the functions you need in the dialogue box.

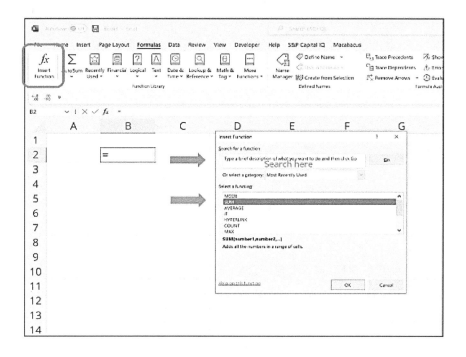

3. Selecting a Formula from One of the Groups in Formula Tab

If you want to go right into your favorite features, this is the way to go. Just click on the Formulas tab and choose the group you want to see this menu in. When you click, a submenu containing a list of functions will be displayed.

Pick the one that suits you best from that menu. If the group you want isn't visible on the tab, try going to the More Functions menu; it's likely hiding somewhere.

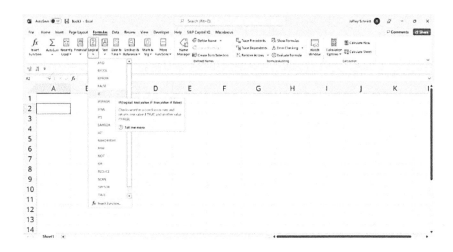

SEVEN BASIC EXCEL FORMULAS FOR YOUR WORKFLOW

So, now that you know how to properly insert your choice formulas into Excel, let's go over some basic functions to get you started.

1. SUM

You should start learning Excel formulas with the SUM function. Typically, it will aggregate values from a subset of the rows or columns in the range you've chosen.

This is the sum of all the numbers from 1 to [number2], inclusive.

To illustrate:

= SUM(B2:G2) - A straightforward option that adds up the values in a row.

=SUM(A2:A8) - A straightforward selection that adds up the numbers in a specific column.

= SUM(A2:A7, A9, A12:A15) - T This complex set adds values from A2–A7, skips A8, adds A9, skips A10–A11, and then adds from A12–A15.

The expression =SUM(A2:A8)/20 demonstrates that your function can also be expressed as a formula.

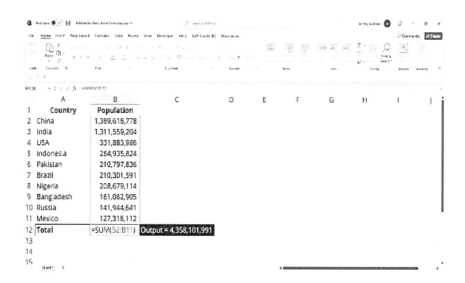

2. AVERAGE

If you're familiar with basic statistics, like the average number of stockholders in a specific pool, you should be familiar with the AVERAGE function.

=AVERAGE(number1, [number2], ...)

Example:

=AVERAGE(B2:B11) – Shows a simple average, also similar to (SUM(B2:B11)/10)

3. COUNT
The COUNT function counts all cells in a given range that contain only numeric values.
=COUNT(value1, [value2], ...)

28

Example:

COUNT(A:A) – Counts all values that are numerical in A column. However, you must adjust the range inside the formula to count rows.

COUNT(A1:C1) – Now it can count rows.

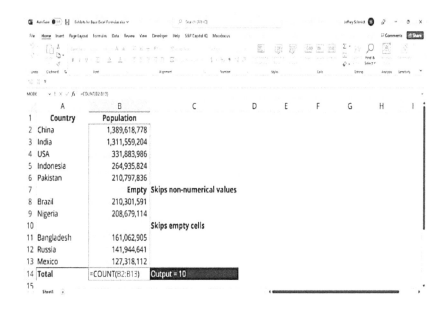

4. COUNTA

Like COUNT, COUNTA counts all cells in a specific rage. But it does a complete count of all cells. In other words, it counts not just numbers but also strings, logical values, dates, times, mistakes, empty strings, and text, in contrast to COUNT, which only counts numbers.

$value1 = COUNTA($value2], $value3...$

To count rows 2–13 in column C, regardless of type, use the following example: COUNTA(C2:C13). But, similar to COUNT, the same algorithm cannot be used to count rows. To modify the selection within the brackets, you can use the following syntax: COUNTA(C2:H2) to count columns C to H.

	A	B	C
1	Country	Population	
2	China	1,389,618,778	
3	India	1,311,559,204	
4	USA	331,883,986	
5	Indonesia	264,935,824	
6	Pakistan	210,797,836	
7		Empty	Counts all entries
8	Brazil	210,301,591	
9	Nigeria	208,679,114	
10			ONLY skips empty cells
11	Bangladesh	161,062,905	
12	Russia	141,944,641	
13	Mexico	127,318,112	
14	Total	=COUNTA(B2:B13)	Output = 11
15			

4. IF

When sorting data according to a specific logic, the IF function is typically employed. The ability to incorporate formulas and functions within the IF formula is its strongest feature.

=IF(logical test, key=True, key=False)

To check if the value at C3 is less than the value at D3, the code uses the =IF(C2<D3,"TRUE","FALSE") condition. Put a TRUE value in the cell if the logic holds. Not true.

= IF(AVERAGE(C1:C10) > AVERAGE(D1:D10), AVERAGE(C1:C10), AVERAGE(D1:D10)) - There is an example of an intricate IF statement. Prior to comparing the sums, it adds up C1 through C10 and D1 through D10. If the total of the columns C1 through C10 is larger than the total of the columns D1 through D10, then the value of a cell is equal to the total of the columns C1 through C10.

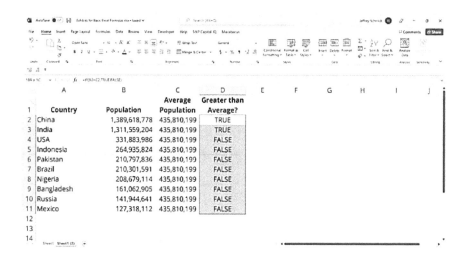

5. TRIM

To prevent your functions from returning incorrect results because of unnecessary gaps in your data, you can use the TRIM function. It checks that there are no blanks. In contrast to other activities, TRIM is cell-specific and can only affect one cell at a time. As a result, you'll end up having duplicate data on your spreadsheet, which is a drawback.

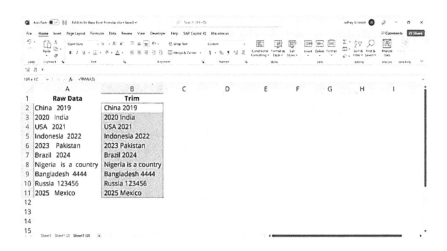

6. MAX & MIN

You can find the highest and lowest values in a range with the aid of the MAX and MIN functions.

is the minimum of the set [number1, [number2],...]

This code finds the lowest value in columns B and C between rows 2 and 11, inclusive, from column B and column C, using the formula =MIN(B2:C11).

iterate through all the numbers from 1 to [number2], and so on.

For instance, when we use =MAX(B2:C11), it finds the highest value between B2 and C2 in column B and C, as well as between B and C, up to row 11.

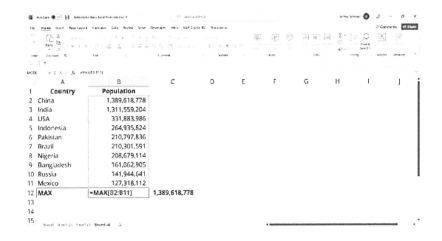

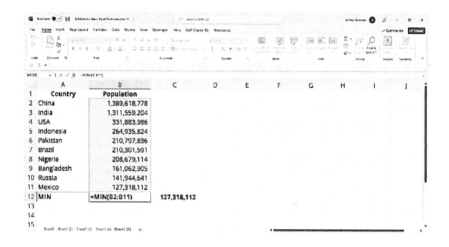

	A	B	C
1	**Country**	**Population**	
2	China	1,389,618,778	
3	India	1,311,559,204	
4	USA	331,883,986	
5	Indonesia	264,935,824	
6	Pakistan	210,797,836	
7	Brazil	210,301,591	
8	Nigeria	208,679,114	
9	Bangladesh	161,062,905	
10	Russia	141,944,641	
11	Mexico	127,318,112	
12	MIN	=MIN(B2:B11)	127,318,112
13			
14			
15			

CHAPTER THREE

STRING (TEXT) FUNCTIONS IN EXCEL

Tabulating and organizing numerical data is often accomplished using Microsoft Excel. On the other hand, it handles text, error, and logical data as well. Every data type in Microsoft Excel has its own special collection of functions. One of Excel's built-in formulas for working with textual data is a text function, often known as an Excel string function.

How To Use Test Functions In Excel

When working with massive amounts of text-based data in Microsoft Excel, text functions are vital for maximizing overall productivity and decreasing handling time. With examples, we'll go over the various Excel text functions.

Left function

With the Left function, you may get the exact number of characters that are on the left side of a text. Using cell B2 as an example, the syntax to extract four letters from the left side of the text would be: =LEFT(B2, 4).

Right function

You can use this method to get characters from the right side of the text, just like the Left function. The following code snippet shows how to get three characters from the right side of the text in cell A2: =RIGHT(A2, 3)

MID function

To get characters at the exact center of a string, you can use the MID text function in Microsoft Excel. Starting with the fifth character, the following syntax can be used to extract seven characters from the middle of the text in B2:

= MID(B2,5,7)

LEN function

You may see how many characters are in a specific cell with this Excel text function. The following is the syntax for the example given below:

the length of B2

FIND function

Using the FIND function, we can see how many characters make up the beginning of the sentence we're trying to find. Take this example of a word like "omelette" as an example; the syntax for finding the position of the letter "tt" is:

found at location "tt" in array B2

The only real difference between Excel's SEARCH and FIND functions is that the former does not care about case sensitivity while the later does.

PROPER function

Capitalizes the initial letter of every word in the chosen cell using the PROPER method. The following is an example of the syntax: =PROPER(B2).

REPT functions

You can get a lot of text repeated with the REPT text function. By applying this procedure three times, the word "Bunny Rabbit" becomes:

is equal to REPT(B2,3)

With this grammar, the text is repeated space-free.

TRIM function

When you use TRIM on a cell, it will eliminate any white space either before or after the text. Here is the syntax for the provided example: =TRIM(B2).

UPPER function

Select a cell and use the UPPER text option to change all the lowercase letters to uppercase. Below is an example of the syntax:

* Raise the value of B2

Lower function

To change all capital letters to lowercase, use this MS Excel text function. In other words, it reverses the effect of the UPPER command. The provided example uses the following syntax: =LOWER(B2).

Substitute function

To insert new text into an existing string, use the SUBSTITUTE function. The two strings must be separated by two inverted commas ("[string]"). For the sake of argument, let's substitute Darwin for Dickens in the following example. Here is the formula for the substitution: =SUBSTITUTE(B2,"Dickens","Darwin")*

Because this function is case-sensitive, it will fail to execute the formula if the input and output texts have different case values.

CONCATENATE Function

To join the text in cells B2, C2, and D2, as shown in the example, you can use the syntax: =CONCATENATE(B2,C2,D2). This will combine the texts from these cells into one cell without spaces. If you want to add a space between the text in two cells, simply type " " (a space enclosed by double inverted commas) between each cell value. In this case, to add spaces, the syntax is: =CONCATENATE(B2," ",C2," ",D2).

DATE FUNCTION IN EXCEL

The primary method for determining dates in Excel:

The DATE method

Find out what time it is right now:

TODAY - the date of return is today

NOW - gives you the exact time and date.

Transform dates into text format:

Using the DATEVALUE function, one can transform a date from text to date format.

TEXT-transforms a date into text format

Get the dates as an Excel chart:

DATE - gives you the current date in leap years

The MONTH function specifies a date and returns that month.

Get the year of a given date with YEAR.

Every month on the last day, EOMONTH returns

WWW - retrieves the current weekday

WEEKNUM - obtains the date's week number

Determine the time gap:

DATEDIF finds the relative age of two dates and returns that value.

EDATE specifies a date that is either N months prior to or after the start date.

Determines the percentage of a year that elapses between two dates using YEARFRAC.

Determine the number of workdays spent:

"WORKDAY" returns a date that is either N working days away or from now. International Time (INTL) - delivers a date N weekdays after the start date with custom weekends

Find out how many business days passed between two dates with NETWORKDAYS.

DAYS OF THENETWORK. find the total number of business days between two dates (including custom weekends) using INTL

You can get the date's serial number by using the DATE function with the year, month, and day parameters.

Knowing how to use the DATE function is crucial if you often deal with dates in Excel. You see, other date functions in Excel aren't always good at recognizing text-based dates. Thus, to get accurate results while calculating dates in Excel, you should input the dates using the DATE function.

Some sample DATE formulas in Excel are shown here:

A serial number associated with May 20, 2015, can be obtained by using the formula =DATE(2015, 5, 20).

Get the current year's and month's first day with the =DATE(YEAR(TODAY()), MONTH(TODAY()), 1) function.

The formula =DATE(2015, 5, 20)-5 removes five days from May 20, 2015.

	A	B	C
1	Formula	Result	Explanation
2	=DATE(2015, 5, 20)	05/20/2015	Returns 20-May-2015
3			
4	=DATE(YEAR(TODAY()), MONTH(TODAY()), 1)	05/01/2015	Returns the 1st day of the
5			current year and month
6	=DATE(2015, 5, 20)-5	05/15/2015	Subtracts 5 days from
7			May 20, 2015

The Excel DATE function has a number of specifics that are highlighted in the Excel DATE tutorial, despite its apparent simplicity at first glance.

The following are some further instances of larger formulas that include the Excel DATE function:

Using Excel to subtract two dates

Date manipulation by adding or removing days

Determine the length of a month.

Excel Today Function:

True to its name, the TODAY method returns the current date.

The lack of arguments in TODAY makes it one of the most user-friendly Excel functions. To get the current date in Excel, just type the following formula into a cell:

= NOW

Beyond this simple application, the Excel TODAY function can be utilized in more intricate computations and formulas that utilize the current date. Put the following formula into a cell to add seven days to the present date, for instance:

The current time plus seven

Use this one to add 30 business days to the current date (not including weekends):

the number of working days is 30 multiplied by the current time

	A	B	C
1	Formula	Result	Explanation
2	=TODAY()	21-May-15	Returns the current date.
3			
4	=TODAY()+7	28-May-15	Adds 7 days to today's date.
5			
6	=WORKDAY(TODAY(), 30)	2-Jul-15	Adds 30 workdays to today's date.

Note: As soon as your spreadsheet is adjusted to reflect the current date, the date given by Excel's TODAY function updates immediately.

EXCEL NOW FUCTION

We may get the current date and time using the NOW method. There are no disputes, just like TODAY. To add the current time and date to your spreadsheet, just insert the following formula into a cell:

Note: Both Excel NOW and TODAY are volatile functions; each time the worksheet is recalculated, the returned value is refreshed. Keep in mind that the NOW formula cell will only get real-time updates when reopening the workbook or performing a new calculation in the worksheet. Pressing Shift+F9 will recalculate the currently active worksheet, or pressing F9 will recalculate all open workbooks. This will cause your NOW formula to update its value.

EXCEL DATEVALUE FUNCTION

The DATEVALUE function takes a date in text format and returns a date-representative serial number.

Both regular date formats and references to cells with "text dates" are understood by the DATEVALUE function. Converting "text dates" to the Date format, as well as calculating, filtering, and sorting them, is a breeze with DATEVALUE.

What follows are some examples of basic DATEVALUE formulas:

=>=DATEVALUE("20-may-2015")
=DATEVALUE("5/20/2015") =DATEVALUE("may 20, 2015")\~

	A	B
1	Formula	Result
2	=DATEVALUE("20-may-2015")	42144
3		
4	=DATEVALUE("5/20/2015")	42144
5		
6	=DATEVALUE("May 20, 2015")	42144

Excel TEXT function

The TEXT function can transform any numerical value into a text string, hence it cannot be considered a date function in Excel.

As shown in the following screenshot, the dates can be converted to text strings in various forms using the TEXT(value, format_text) method.

	A	B	C
1	Date	Formula	Result
2	5/20/2015	=TEXT(A2,"d-mmm-yy")	20-May-15
3			
4		=TEXT(A2,"dd mmmm, yyyy")	20 May, 2015
5			
6		=TEXT(A2,"dddd, mmmm d, yyyy")	Wednesday, May 20, 2015

Note: You can't use the results of the TEXT function in any other computations or formulas, even though they seem like regular Excel dates—they're just text values.

Excel DAY function

The DAY function takes a serial number and returns an integer between 1 and 31 representing the day of the month.

If you want to know what day of the week it is, you can find it in serial number. Possible values include cell references, dates input via the DATE function, or output from other calculations.

A couple of instances of formulas are these:

DAY(DATE(2015,1,1)) provides the current day of the month based on the date in A2. - tomorrow, January 1, 2015

TODAY = DAY returns the current day of the year.

	A	B	C	D
1	Date	Formula	Result	Explanation
2	1-Jan-15	=DAY(A2)	1	Returns the day of the date in A2
3				
4		=DAY(DATE(2015,1,1))	1	Returns the day of 1-Jan-2015
5				
6		=DAY(TODAY())	20	Returns the day of today's date

Excel MONTH function

The month of a given date can be obtained as an integer between 1 (January) and 12 (December) using Excel's MONTH(serial number) function.

Take this case in point:

The formula =MONTH(A2) finds out what month a date in cell A2 is in.

To get the current month, use the formula =MONTH(TODAY()).

47

When working with dates in Excel, the MONTH function is not often used alone. As you can see in the following examples, it is most commonly used in conjunction with other functions.

Excel YEAR function

You can get the year that corresponds to a given date as a number between 1900 and 9999 by calling YEAR(serial number).

When calculating dates in Excel, you should have little trouble using the YEAR function because it is so simple:

Get the year of a date in cell A2 with the =YEAR(A2) function.

The year of the given date can be obtained by using the =YEAR("20-May-2015") function.

=YEAR(DATE(2015,5,20))—a more trustworthy way to obtain the year of a certain date.

To get the current year, use the formula =YEAR(TODAY()).

	A	B	C	D
1	Date	Formula	Result	Explanation
2	20-May-15	=YEAR(A2)	2015	Returns the year of a date in cell A2.
3				
4		=YEAR("20-May-2015")	2015	Return the year of a specified date (20-May-2015).
5				
6		=YEAR(DATE(2015,5,20))	2015	
7				
8		=YEAR(TODAY())	2015	Return the current year.

Excel WEEKDAY function

The WEEKDAY function takes a serial number and returns the day of the week from 1 (Sunday) to 7 (Saturday) as a number.

You can pass in a date, a cell reference to a date, or the date returned by another Excel function as serial number.

You can choose which day of the week is to be considered the first by using the optional parameter return type, which is a number.

Additionally, I have included some WEEKEND formula examples:

The formula =WEEKDAY(A2) provides the current day of the week for a given date in cell A2. By default, Sunday is the first day of the week.

If you enter a date in cell A2, the formula =WEEKDAY(A2, 2) will return Monday as the day of the week.

The current day of the week is represented by the integer returned by =WEEKDAY(TODAY()); the week starts on Sunday.

	A	B	C	D
1	Start date	Formula	Result	Explanation
2	1-Jan-13	=DATEDIF(A2, B5, "m")	28	Complete months between dates in A2 and B2.
3				
4	End date	=DATEDIF(A2, B5, "y")	2	Complete years between dates in A2 and B2.
5	20-May-15			
6		=DATEDIF(A2, TODAY(), "d")	870	Days between the date in A2 and today's date.

Excel DATEDIF function

The purpose of the DATEDIF(start date, end date, unit) function is to determine the time interval between two dates in terms of days, months, or years.

Depending on the letter you input in the last argument, the time period to be used for computing the date difference is:

The number of days between the date in A2 and today's date is calculated using the formula =DATEDIF(A2, TODAY(), "d").

The number of full months that have passed between dates A2 and B2 can be found using the formula =DATEDIF(A2, A5, "m").

=DATEDIF(A2, A5, "y") - finds the total number of years that have passed between A2 and B2 of the specified dates.

	A	B	C	D
1	Start date	Formula	Result	Explanation
2	1-Jan-13	=DATEDIF(A2, B5, "m")	28	Complete months between dates in A2 and B2.
3				
4	End date	=DATEDIF(A2, B5, "y")	2	Complete years between dates in A2 and B2.
5	20-May-15			
6		=DATEDIF(A2, TODAY(), "d")	870	Days between the date in A2 and today's date.

TIME FUNCTION IN EXCEL

You can find the TIME Function[1] under the Excel DATE/TIME functions category. TIME allows us to construct a time with distinct components for the hour, minute, and second.

It could be helpful to include a time stamp on reports while undertaking financial analyses. In these cases, you can use TIME to transform a string of text into a decimal representation of the time. Combining multiple values into one time value is another possible usage of the function.

Formula

=TIME(hour, minute, second)

The time function use the following arguments:

1. The hour can be any integer between zero and three hundred twenty-seven, which is the required parameter. If the amount is greater than 23, Excel will divide it by 24 to get the hour value.
2. The minute is a mandatory argument that can take on any value between zero and three hundred twenty-seven. We convert numbers to hours and minutes if they are more than 59.

3. Second (mandatory argument) — It may take on any value between 0 (zero) and 32767 (the number of seconds). Time units of hours, minutes, and seconds are applied to any value greater than 59.

How to use the TIME Function in Excel

You can use TIME as a formula component in a worksheet cell since it is a worksheet function.

Here are a few examples to help you understand how the TIME function is used:

- Imagine we obtained the following information by extracting it from a PDF file:

	A	B	C	D
1				
2		TIME Function		
3				
4		Hour	Minute	Second
5		9	0	0
6		12	30	5
7		24	0	-1.00
8		6	75	5
9		18	-1	0

Using the TIME function, we can now insert the time into the cell itself. Instead of using TIME(hour, minutes, seconds), you should use =TIME(B5,C5,D5).

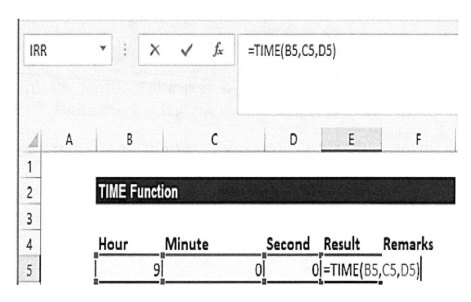

We get the results below:

| E5 | | | ✕ | ✓ | f_x | =TIME(B5,C5,D5) |

⊿	A	B	C	D	E	F
1						
2		**TIME Function**				
3						
4		Hour	Minute		Second	Result	Remarks
5		9	0		0	9:00 AM	
6		12	30		5	12:30 PM	
7		24	0		-1.00	11:59 PM	
8		6	75		5	7:15 AM	
9		18	-1		0	5:59 PM	

In row 4, the hours are 24, which is greater than 23. Any value greater than 23 will be divided by 24, with the remainder treated as the hour value. In this case, 24 would be 00. Then, we got -1 as seconds, which is negative, so it was subtracted to give 11:59. Keep in mind that if the second argument is negative or greater than 59, the time extends back into the previous or following minute. If the minute argument is negative or greater than 59, the time extends back into the previous or following hour. In row 6, we get 5:59 pm.

- You can use the TIME function, add hours, divide by 24, or any other method to add time to a given number of hours. Let us pretend we have the following information:

55

	A	B	C
1			
2		**TIME Function**	
3			
4		Time	Hours
5		12:00:00 AM	5
6		12:00:00 AM	6
7		12:00:00 AM	12
8		12:00:00 AM	24
9		12:00:00 AM	30

In order to get the total number of hours, we can utilize the TIME function. We don't have to keep track of the formula to convert decimal hours to an Excel time; the function does it for us. In this case, the correct formula is =A2+TIME(B2,0,0).

We get the results below:

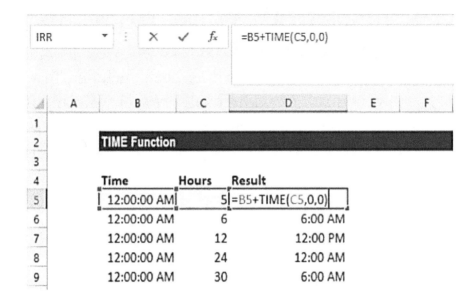

| IRR | ▼ | : | × | ✓ | fx | =B5+TIME(C5,0,0) |

▲	A	B	C	D	E	F
1						
2		**TIME Function**				
3						
4		Time	Hours	Result		
5		12:00:00 AM	5	=B5+TIME(C5,0,0)		
6		12:00:00 AM	6	6:00 AM		
7		12:00:00 AM	12	12:00 PM		
8		12:00:00 AM	24	12:00 AM		
9		12:00:00 AM	30	6:00 AM		

As you can see in rows 5 and 6, the TIME function will "roll over" to zero when the value exceeds 24 hours.

Our method for subtracting hours from a given time is =MOD(A2-TIME(B2,0,0),1).

If you have any problems with negative values, the MOD function can handle them. In order to get the desired positive numbers, MOD will "flip" negative ones.

THINGS TO REMEMBER ABOUT THE TIME FUNCTION

- The TIME function has been included in all versions of Microsoft Excel since its introduction in 2000.
- The #NUM! error happens when the provided hour arguments result in a negative time, meaning they are less than zero.
- The #VALUE! error happens whenever one of the inputs is not a number.

CHAPTER FOUR

LOGICAL FEATURES IN EXCEL

To manipulate logical values, Microsoft Excel has four built-in functions. You can use AND, OR, XOR, and NOT as functions. When you need to compare more than one variable in your calculation or test more than one condition at a time, these functions come in handy. Excel logical functions, like logical operators, analyze arguments and return TRUE or FALSE.

To assist you in selecting the appropriate formula for a given assignment, the following table gives a brief description of each logical function and what it performs.

Function	Description	Formula Example	Formula Description
AND	Returns TRUE if all of the arguments evaluate to TRUE.	=AND (A2>=10, B2<5)	The formula returns TRUE if a value in cell A2 is greater than or equal to 10, and a value in B2 is less than 5, FALSE otherwise.
OR	Returns TRUE if any argument evaluates to TRUE.	=OR (A2>=10, B2<5)	The formula returns TRUE if A2 is greater than or equal to 10 or B2 is less than 5, or both conditions are met. If neither of the conditions it met, the formula returns FALSE.
XOR	Returns a logical Exclusive Or of all arguments.	=XOR (A2>=10, B2<5)	The formula returns TRUE if either A2 is greater than or equal to 10 or B2 is less than 5. If neither of the conditions is met or both conditions are met, the formula returns FALSE.
NOT	Returns the reversed logical value of its argument. I.e. If the argument is FALSE, then TRUE is returned and vice versa.	=NOT (A2>=10)	The formula returns FALSE if a value in cell A1 is greater than or equal to 10; TRUE otherwise.

There are three more "conditional" functions available in Microsoft Excel beyond the four logical functions mentioned earlier: IF, IFERROR, and IFNA.

Excel logical functions - facts and figures

1. Excel functions such as cell references, text and numeric values, Boolean values, comparison operators, and more can be used as parameters to logical functions. The only

valid argument types are those that include logical values, such as pointers or arrays, or the Boolean values TRUE or FALSE.

2. Any empty cells in a logical function's argument will have their values disregarded. The formula will return the #VALUE! error if any of the arguments are cells that are empty.

3. When numbers are part of a logical function's input, the value of zero is FALSE and the value of any other number, even negative values, is TRUE. The formula =AND(A1:A5) will return TRUE if no cell in A1:A5 contains 0, and FALSE otherwise, given that cells A1–A5 contain numbers.

4. If an argument does not evaluate to a logical value, the #VALUE! error will be returned by the logical function.

5. The #NAME? problem occurs when trying to utilize a logical function in an older version of Excel that does not support it or when the function's name is misspelled. As an example, you can only use the XOR function on Excel 2016 and 2013.

6. As long as the formula doesn't go beyond 8,192 characters, you can use up to 255 arguments in a logical function in Excel 2007 and later. You are limited to 30 parameters

and a maximum of 1,024 characters in Excel 2003 and earlier formulas.

Using the AND function in Excel

In the realm of logic functions, the AND function reigns supreme. If you need to check that multiple conditions are satisfied, it's a lifesaver. In mathematic terms, the AND function takes a set of criteria and returns TRUE if every one of them is true and FALSE otherwise.

The syntax for the Excel AND function is as follows:

The condition you wish to test can be evaluated as TRUE or FALSE; this is where logic comes in. You must meet the first criterion (logical1) in order to continue; all other conditions are discretionary.

Now that we know how to use the AND functions in Excel, let's examine some formula examples.

Formula	Description
=AND(A2="Bananas", B2>C2)	Returns TRUE if A2 contains "Bananas" and B2 is greater than C2, FALSE otherwise.
=AND(B2>20, B2=C2)	Returns TRUE if B2 is greater than 20 and B2 is equal to C2, FALSE otherwise.
=AND(A2="Bananas", B2>=30, B2>C2)	Returns TRUE if A2 contains "Bananas", B2 is greater than or equal to 30 and B2 is greater than C2, FALSE otherwise.

	A	B	C	D	E	F
1	Product	In Stock	Sold	Formula 1	Formula 2	Formula 3
2				=AND(A2="Bananas", B2>C1)	=AND(B2>20, B2=C2)	=AND(A2="Bananas", B2>=30, B2>C2)
3	Bananas	30	20	TRUE	FALSE	TRUE
4	Oranges	40	40	FALSE	TRUE	FALSE
5	Bananas	20	20	FALSE	FALSE	FALSE
6	Oranges	40	10	FALSE	FALSE	FALSE

Excel AND function - common uses

The AND function in Excel is boring and only useful in certain contexts when used alone. But when you use AND with other Excel functions, your spreadsheets' possibilities can be greatly expanded.

The logical test parameter of the IF function is a popular place to employ the AND function in Excel for testing multiple conditions at once, rather than just one. To obtain an outcome comparable to this, you can nest any of the AND functions mentioned earlier within the IF function:

=IF(AND(A2="Bananas", B2>C2), "Good", "Bad")

| | D2 | ▼ | ⋮ | ✕ ✓ _fx_ | =IF(AND(A2="Bananas", B2>C2), "Good", "Bad") |

	A	B	C	D
1	Product	In Stock	Sold	IF formula
2	Bananas	30	20	Good
3	Oranges	40	40	Bad
4	Bananas	20	20	Bad
5	Oranges	40	10	Bad

An Excel formula for the BETWEEN condition

For situations where you need to create an Excel formula that selects all values between two given values, one common method is to use the IF function with AND in the logical test. For instance, if you have three values in columns A, B, and C and you want to determine if a value in column A falls between B and C values, you can simply use the IF function with nested AND and a couple of comparison operators:

Formula to check if X is between Y and Z, inclusive:

=IF(AND(A2>=B2,A2<=C2),"Yes", "No")

Formula to check if X is between Y and Z, not inclusive:

=IF(AND(A2>B2, A2<C2),"Yes", "No")

	Is between Values 2 and 3?	Lower-bound value	Upper-bound value	
	↓	↓	↓	
	A	B	C	D
1	Value 1	Value 2	Value 3	Is Value 1 between Value 2 & Value 3?
2				=IF(AND(A2>=B2,A2<=C2),"Yes", "No")
3	5	1	10	Yes
4	10	6	8	No
5	4	2	5	Yes
6	12	15	3	No
7	7-Oct	5-Oct	27-Oct	Yes
8	24-Nov	26-Dec	21-Oct	No
9	13-Oct	13-Oct	17-Oct	Yes
10	Bananas	Apples	Cherries	Yes
11	Apples	Apricot	Bananas	No

Numbers, dates, and text values are all flawlessly handled by the formula, as shown in the screenshot above. The formula compares text values alphabetically, character by character. The rule says that apples aren't in the same category as apricots and bananas, for instance, because the second "p" in apples comes before the "r" in apricots.

The IF/AND formula is quick, easy, and practically applicable in almost every situation. I say "almost" because it doesn't address a single possible situation. Column B always includes the lower bound value and column C - the upper bound value, according to the aforementioned formula. This is why row 6 (A6, 12, B6, 15, and C6) and row 8 (A8, 24, 26, and Oct.) both get "No" from the formula.

What if, however, you would need your between formula to remain accurate independent of the values of the lower and higher bounds? Here, you may find the middle number (the median) in the provided numbers by using the MEDIAN function in Excel.

Thus, the expression will look like this when you substitute MEDIAN for AND in the logical test of the IF function:

where A2 is the median of A2 with respect to C2, and "Yes" and "No" are the possible outcomes.

And you will get the following results:

	A	B	C	D
1	Value 1	Value 2	Value 3	Is Value 1 between Value 2 & Value 3?
2				=IF(A2=MEDIAN(A2:C2),"Yes","No")
3	5	1	10	Yes
4	10	6	8	No
5	4	2	5	Yes
6	12	15	3	Yes
7	7-Oct	5-Oct	27-Oct	Yes
8	24-Nov	26-Dec	21-Oct	Yes
9	13-Oct	13-Oct	17-Oct	Yes
10	Bananas	Apples	Cherries	#NUM!
11	Apples	Apricot	Bananas	#NUM!

Despite its flawless performance with dates and numbers, the MEDIAN function consistently returns the #NUM! mismatch between text values and validation. Unfortunately, nobody is faultless :)

If you're looking for an ideal Between formula that can handle text values in addition to numbers and dates, you'll need to build a more intricate logical text utilizing the AND/OR operations, such as this:

If the condition "Yes" or "No" is true, then the expression is true.

	A	B	C	D	E
	Value 1	Value 2	Value 3	Is Value 1 between Value 2 and Value 3?	
2	5	1	10	Yes	
3	5-Oct	6-Oct	5-Sep	Yes	
4	Bananas	Apples	Cherries	Yes	
5	Apples	Apricot	Bananas	No	

D2   ▼   :   ✕ ✓ f_x =IF(OR(AND(A2>B2, A2<C2), AND(A2<B2, A2>C2)),"Yes", "No")

Using the OR function in Excel

Another fundamental logical tool for comparing values or phrases is the OR function in Excel. It works similarly to the AND function. In contrast, if either one of the parameters evaluates to TRUE, the OR function will return TRUE; otherwise, it will return FALSE. You may use the OR function in Excel 2016 all the way back to 2000.

The syntax of the Excel OR function is very similar to AND:

OR(logical1, [logical2], ...)

Where logical is an assertion that you wish to verify as true or false. All conditions except the first logical are optional; newer versions of Excel allow up to 255.

For your convenience, let's jot down some formulas to demonstrate how the OR function in Excel is used.

Formula	Description
=OR(A2="Bananas", A2="Oranges")	Returns TRUE if A2 contains "Bananas" or "Oranges", FALSE otherwise.
=OR(B2>=40, C2>=20)	Returns TRUE if B2 is greater than or equal to 40 or C2 is greater than or equal to 20, FALSE otherwise.
=OR(B2=" ", C2="")	Returns TRUE if either B2 or C2 is blank or both, FALSE otherwise.

	A	B	C	D	E	F
1	Product	In Stock	Sold	Formula 1	Formula 2	Formula 3
2				=OR(A2="Bananas", A2="Oranges")	=OR(B2>=40, C2>=20)	=OR(B2="", C2="")
3	Bananas	30	10	TRUE	FALSE	FALSE
4	Oranges		20	TRUE	TRUE	TRUE
5	Cherries	20		FALSE	FALSE	TRUE
6	Oranges	30	10	TRUE	FALSE	FALSE
7	Cherries			FALSE	FALSE	TRUE

In addition to the AND function, the OR function is commonly utilized to enhance the functionality of other Excel functions that conduct logical tests, such as the IF function. A few examples are shown here:

IF Function With Nested OR

IF (B2>30 AND C2>20) THEN "Good" AND "Bad"

In this case, the formula will return "Good" since cell B3 has a number more than 30 or "Bad" since cell C2 contains a number greater than 20.

Excel AND / OR Functions In One Formula

If your business logic demands it, there's no problem using both AND and OR in a single formula. These formulas can take on an endless variety of forms, all of which share commonalities:

Consider the following expressions: =AND(OR(Cond1, Cond2), Cond3), OR(Cond3, Cond4), OR(AND(Cond1, Cond2), Cond3), OR(AND(Cond1, Cond2), AND(Cond3,Cond4).

If you were interested in seeing which banana and orange consignments were sold out—that is, if the "In stock" number (column B) was equal to the "Sold" number (column C)—you could get that information fast using the following OR/AND formula:

if (A2="bananas" and B2=C2) and (A2="oranges" and B2=C2) are both true, then.

E2	▾	:	✕	✓	f_x	=OR(AND(A2="bananas", B2=C2), AND(A2="oranges", B2=C2))

	A	B	C	D	E	F
1	Product	In Stock	Sold	Supplier	Bananas & oranges sold out	
2	Apples	40	30	Peter	FALSE	
3	Bananas	30	20	Josh	FALSE	
4	Oranges	40	40	Peter	TRUE	
5	Bananas	30	20	Peter	FALSE	
6	Oranges	40	10	Josh	FALSE	
7	Bananas	50	50	Josh	TRUE	

=OR($B2="", $C2="") in Excel's conditional formatting

Rows containing an empty cell in column B, column C, or both are highlighted by the rule using the aforementioned OR algorithm.

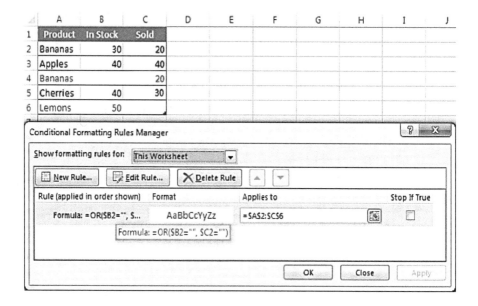

Using the XOR function in Excel

The XOR function, short for "logical exclusive OR," was introduced in Excel 2013 by Microsoft. For individuals who are knowledgeable with computer science or any programming language, this term will be immediately recognizable. The following explanation, along by formula examples, should help individuals who don't understand what "Exclusive Or" means.

The syntax of the XOR function is identical to OR's :

XOR(logical1, [logical2],...)

You can test up to 254 conditions in one formula, and the first logical statement (Logical 1) is obligatory; additional logical values are optional. They can be arrays, references, or logical values that evaluate to TRUE or FALSE.

In the simplest version, an XOR formula contains just 2 logical statements and returns:

- It is true if and only if both arguments are true.
- NOT TRUE if either of the arguments is true but not both.

This might be easier to understand from the formula examples:

Formula	Result	Description
=XOR(1>0, 2<1)	TRUE	Returns TRUE because the 1st argument is TRUE and the 2nd argument is FALSE.
=XOR(1<0, 2<1)	FALSE	Returns FALSE because both arguments are FALSE.
=XOR(1>0, 2>1)	FALSE	Returns FALSE because both arguments are TRUE.

The XOR function in Excel produces the following outcomes when additional logical statements are added:

If there are an odd number of arguments that evaluate to TRUE, then the statement is true. Otherwise, it is false.

The screenshot below illustrates the point:

	A	B	C	D	E	F
F1					f_x	=XOR(A1:E1)
1	TRUE	TRUE	TRUE	TRUE	TRUE	TRUE
2	FALSE	TRUE	TRUE	TRUE	TRUE	FALSE
3	FALSE	FALSE	TRUE	TRUE	TRUE	TRUE
4	FALSE	FALSE	FALSE	TRUE	TRUE	FALSE
5	FALSE	FALSE	FALSE	FALSE	TRUE	TRUE
6	FALSE	FALSE	FALSE	FALSE	FALSE	FALSE

If you're unsure about how to use the Excel XOR function in a practical situation, have a look at this example. Assume you have a table with the participants and the outcomes of the first two games. You wish to choose which payer, under the following circumstances, will participate in the third game:

- Participants who win Games 1 and 2 immediately move on to the next round and do not need to play Games 3 or 4.
- Those who lose their first two games are eliminated and do not participate in Game 3.

- The winners of Games 1 and 2 will compete in Game 3 to decide who advances to the next round and who does not.

An easy XOR formula does just what we need it to:

(B2="Won", C2="Won") =XOR

| D2 ▼ : ✕ ✓ f_x | =XOR(B2="Won", C2="Won") |

	A	B	C	D
1	Contestant	Game 1	Game 2	Play Game 3?
2	Andrew	Won	Won	FALSE
3	Billy	Won	Lost	TRUE
4	Erik	Lost	Won	TRUE
5	Josh	Lost	Lost	FALSE

Additionally, you will obtain even more logical results if you nest this XOR function inside the IF formula's logical test:

=IF("Yes", "No"), XOR(B2="Won", C2="Won")

D2		=IF(XOR(B2="Won", C2="Won"), "Yes", "No")

	A	B	C	D	E
1	Contestant	Game 1	Game 2	Play Game 3?	
2	Andrew	Won	Won	No	
3	Billy	Won	Lost	Yes	
4	Erik	Lost	Won	Yes	
5	Josh	Lost	Lost	No	

Using The NOT Function In Excel

The NOT function is one of the simplest Excel functions in terms of syntax:

NOT(logical)

Excel's NOT function can be used to reverse an argument's value. Put differently, the NOT function returns TRUE if logic evaluates to FALSE and vice versa. For instance, the following two formulas both yield FALSE:

Equal to NOT(TRUE) = NOT(2*2=4)

Why would someone seek such absurd outcomes? Sometimes, knowing when a particular condition is met rather than when it isn't may pique your curiosity more. For instance, you might want to cross out any color that doesn't go well with you when going through a list of outfit ideas. Since I don't like black too much, I use the following formula: =NOT(C2="black")

| E2 | | | | f_x | =NOT(C2="black") |

	A	B	C	D	E
1	Item	Description	Color	Price	Any color but black
2	113456	Coat	White	$980	TRUE
3	113457	Coat	Black	$1,090	FALSE
4	113458	Jacket	Brown	$780	TRUE
5	113459	Fur coat	White	$1,000	TRUE
6	113460	Fur coat	Ivory	$1,035	TRUE
7	113461	Jacket	Black	$760	FALSE
8	113462	Coat	White	$800	TRUE

As usual, there are other ways to do tasks in Microsoft Excel. The Not equal to operator can be used to get the same outcome: =C2<>"black".

You can use NOT in conjunction with the AND or OR function to test many conditions in a single formula. For instance, the formula would be =NOT(OR(C2="black", C2="white")) if you wished to omit the colors black and white.

If you would like not to own a black coat, you can use the Excel AND function in conjunction with NOT to avoid having a black coat or a fur coat on the back.

=NOT(AND("black", "coat", C2="black"))

Reversing the behavior of another function is another popular use for Excel's NOT function. For example, you can develop the ISNOTBLANK formula that Microsoft Excel does not have by combining the NOT and ISBLANK functions.

As you are aware, if cell A2 is blank, the formula =ISBLANK(A2) yields TRUE. This outcome can be changed to FALSE using the NOT function: =NOT(ISBLANK(A2))

Next, for a practical task, you may go one step further and construct a nested IF statement using the NOT and ISBLANK functions:

*0.15, C2*IF(NOT(ISBLANK(C2)), "No bonus:(")

D2		:	=IF(NOT(ISBLANK(C2)), C2*0.15, "No bonus :(")

	A	B	C	D	E
1	Salesman	Primary sales	Extra sales	Bonus	
2	Andrew	$1,860	$169	$25	
3	Billy	$910	$145	$22	
4	Erik	$1,020		No bonus :(	
5	Josh	$1,070	$185	$28	
6	Mike	$1,100		No bonus :(	
7	Steve	$1,020	$180	$27	

Put simply, the formula instructs Excel to perform the following actions. If cell C2 is not empty, multiply the value there by 0.15 to award each salesman who has made any more sales with a 15% bonus. The text "No bonus :(" displays if C2 is blank.

This is essentially how Excel's logical functions are used. Of fact, these are only a few instances of the many uses for AND, OR, XOR, and NOT. Now that you know the fundamentals, you may build on your understanding by taking on your actual chores and creating clever, complex formulas for your spreadsheets.

MATH FEATURES IN EXCEL

Numerous built-in functions for calculating numerical data are available in Excel's Mathematical Functions. Common functions include SUM, AVERAGE, COUNT, MIN, MAX, and many more.

You may find the Mathematical Functions in the Math & Trig functions group, which is located under the Formula tab.

With the Mathematical MAX Excel Function, we may discover the maximum value in cells with numbers in column A, as seen in cell A7 of the following figure.

	A
1	Value
2	23
3	12
4	67
5	2
6	40
7	?
8	

=MAX(A2:A6)

The output comes as '67'.

A7	▾	⋮	✕	✓	*fx*	=MAX(A2:A6)

	A	B	C	D	E
1	Value				
2	23				
3	12				
4	67				
5	2				
6	40				
7	67				
8					

7 Math Functions Used In MS Excel

1. Sum

A user can use the SUM function in Excel to add numerical numbers, cell references, ranges, or all three at once with the formula =SUM. In the same way, adding all the numerical values in a specific row or column is done automatically when you use Excel's Auto Sum function, which is "Σ".

The syntax of the SUM Excel formula is

Mathematical Function in Excel - SUM Formula Syntax

81

Number 1 =The first numerical value you wish to insert. This argument must be made.

Number 2 =The second numerical value you would like to provide. An optional argument, this is it.

A sequence of numbers from 10 to 100 is shown in the picture below as an example. The mathematical SUM function will be used to add up the values.

The table includes

- The value in Column A is the sum of all
- You can find the output in Column B.

The following are the steps to add the provided numbers:

- First step :Picking the cell that will display the outcome is the first step. In this scenario, it would be Cell B2.

	A	B
1	Number	Output
2	10	?
3	20	
4	30	
5	40	
6	50	
7	60	
8	70	
9	80	
10	90	
11	100	
12		

- Second Step: After that, go to cell B2 and type in the SUM formula.
- Third step choose an array that contains the addresses of all the cells in the table, from the first to the last (A2:A11).
- Fourth Step: The whole formula that has to be entered is =SUM(A2:A11).

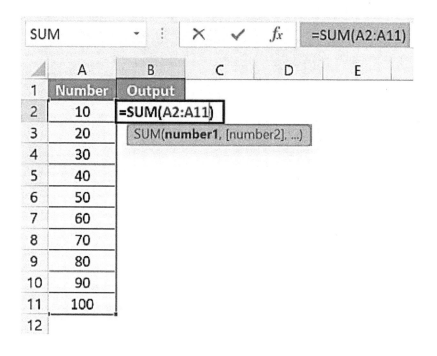

| SUM | ▼ ⋮ | ✕ ✓ f_x | =SUM(A2:A11) |

	A	B	C	D	E
1	Number	Output			
2	10	=SUM(A2:A11)			
3	20	SUM(**number1**, [number2], ...)			
4	30				
5	40				
6	50				
7	60				
8	70				
9	80				
10	90				
11	100				
12					

step 5 :press the Enter key. In the figure below, the results are displayed in cell B2 as 550.

| B2 | | | | | | | f_x | =SUM(A2:A11) |

	A	B	C	D	E
1	Number	Output			
2	10	550			
3	20				
4	30				
5	40				
6	50				
7	60				
8	70				
9	80				
10	90				
11	100				
12					

2. Average

By passing in a set of numbers as parameters, Excel's AVERAGE function determines their mathematical mean. You can pass in numbers as parameters or use cell references that include numbers.

The syntax of the AVERAGE Excel formula is

Mathematical Function in Excel - AVERAGE Formula Syntax

number1 is the first numerical value used to compute the average. This argument must be made.

"number2" is the second integer that will be averaged. An optional argument, this is it.

Fruit prices are shown in the picture below as an example. Using the mathematical AVERAGE function, we will endeavor to determine the average of the figures.

- The fruits are listed in column A of the table.
- You may find the price in Column B.
- The Output is located in Cell B7.

Following these procedures will allow you to determine the average of the provided numbers:

Step 1: select the cell where you'd like the output to show up. In this scenario, the cell in question would be B7.

	A	B
1	**Fruits**	**Price**
2	Lemon	100
3	Banana	50
4	Apple	250
5	Peach	200
6	Kiwi	50
7	**Average**	?
8		

- Step 2, in cell B7, we shall input the AVERAGE formula.
- In step 3, choose the cell reference (B2:B6) from the table.
- Step 4: The whole formula that has to be entered is =AVERAGE(B2:B6).

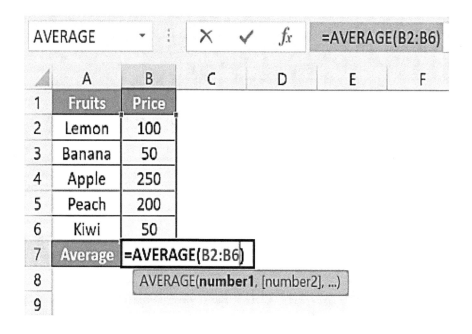

Step 5, hit the Enter key. In the figure below, the result is displayed as '130' in cell B7.

3. AVERAGEIF

In Excel, you can find the mathematical mean of all the integers in a range of cells using the AVERAGEIF Function. It takes various criteria into account.

The AVERAGEIF formula in Excel is

Mathematical Function in Excel - AVERAGEIF Formula Syntax

- range= This parameter must be present. This range should be used to apply the related criteria.
- criterion=The criteria argument must be present. These are the standards that should be used to evaluate the corresponding range.
- The optional argument is average_range. We would like to average these cells.

The picture below shows products and their sales figures as an example. Using the Mathematical AVEARGEIF function, we shall determine the average based on these values' criteria.

In the table,

- Column A displays the Items
- Sales data is presented in Column B.
- Cell C2 houses the end product

To find the mean of the provided numbers, perform these steps:

First step: select the cell where you'd like the output to show up. Here, the cell in question would be Cell C2.

	A	B	C
1	Items	Sales	Average Sale of Lemon Tart
2	Lemon Tart	100	?
3	Banana	50	
4	Apple Pie	250	
5	Lemon Tart	200	
6	Cakes	50	
7	Pear	60	
8	Lemon Tart	90	
9	Pancakes	80	
10			

step 2: in cell C2, we shall input the AVERAGEIF formula.

Step 3: Choose a value that falls between the range of cell addresses in the table, which is A2:A9.

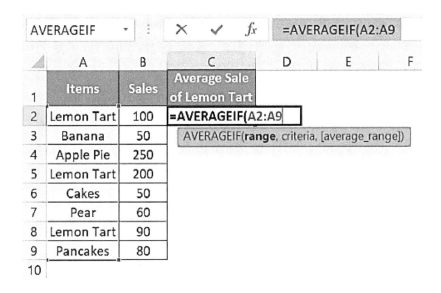

- Step 4: decide what we're going to use as our metric; in this case, lemon tart.

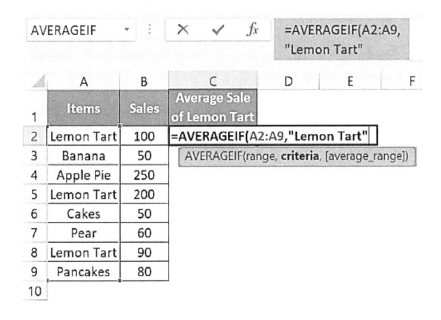

- step 5:choose the average range, which is the range from B2 to B9, the addresses of the first and last cells in the table.
- step 6 :you must input the full formula: =AVERAGEIF(A2:A9, "Lemon Tart," B2:B9).The fifth step is to choose the average range, which is the range from B2 to B9 (the beginning and ending cell addresses of the list).

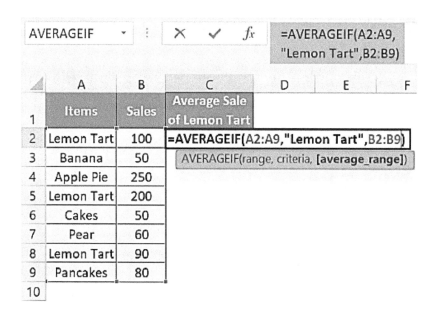

Step7: Hit the Enter key. The output in cell C2 is shown as '130' in the figure below.

| C2 | | ▼ | ⋮ | × | ✓ | *fx* | =AVERAGEIF(A2:A9, "Lemon Tart",B2:B9) |

	A	B	C	D	E	F
1	Items	Sales	Average Sale of Lemon Tart			
2	Lemon Tart	100	130			
3	Banana	50				
4	Apple Pie	250				
5	Lemon Tart	200				
6	Cakes	50				
7	Pear	60				
8	Lemon Tart	90				
9	Pancakes	80				
10						

In light of this, the AVERAGEIF function determines the mean based on the parameters. Here is the value of "Lemon Tart" when the requirements are checked in the manual computation of the average:

Add 100, 200, and 90 to get 390.

The average is 130, with 390 divided by the total number of values.

4. Count

In Excel, you can find out how many cells have numbers in a specific range by using the COUNT function. Another thing this function does is tally up how many arguments contain numerical values.

The syntax of the COUNT Excel formula is

Mathematical Function in Excel - COUNT Formula Syntax

- value1 = The range to be counted or the first cell reference. This argument must be made.
- value2= The range to be counted or the second cell reference. An optional argument, this is it.

The picture below shows values in several forms as an example. Starting in cell B2, we will attempt to use the Mathematical COUNT formula to count the cells that have numerical values.

In the table,

- Column A shows values
- Cell B2 calculates the number of numeric values

The following are the steps to add the provided numbers:

- Step one: select the cell where you'd like the output to show up. In this scenario, it would be Cell B2.

	A	B
1	Values	Output
2	1000	?
3	$6755	
4	2222	
5	346a	
6	abcd	
7	$4,55,378	
8		

- Step two: is to go to cell B2 and type in the COUNT formula.
- Step three: choose an array that contains the addresses of all the cells in the table, from the first to the last (A2:A7).
- Step four: The whole formula that has to be entered is =COUNT(A2:A7).

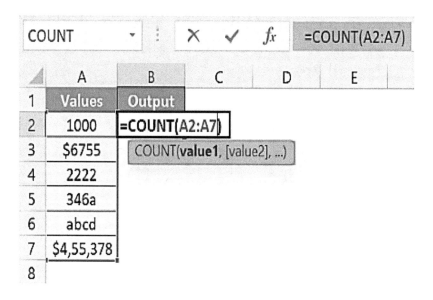

- Step five: hit the Enter key. In the figure below, the findings in cell B2 are shown as '2'.

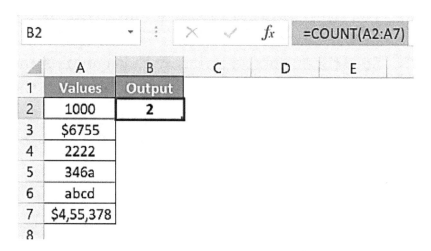

- Hence, the COUNT function does not take variables into account when counting numbers it merely counts numbers as numerical values.

5. COUNTIF

In Excel, you can use the COUNTIF function to get the total number of cells that meet certain criteria within a specified range.

The syntax of the COUNTIF Excel formula is

Mathematical Function in Excel - COUNTIF Formula Syntax

- Range=The criteria argument is applied to this range. This argument must be presented.
- Criteria=The range of values argument is subject to this condition. This argument must be presented.

The graphic below serves as an illustration of how the tasks are assigned to individuals. Here, we'll use Excel's Mathematical COUNTIF function to see whether we can get the total number of members in the tasks listed in the table.

In the table,

- Shown in Column A is the Name
- The Task is located in Column B.

- The output is located in column E.

Following these procedures will allow you to determine the number of cells that meet the criteria:

- Step 1, we'll select the column that will display the result. In this instance, the corresponding column would be E.

	A	B	C	D	E
1	Name	Task		Count the values with COUNTIF	
2	Albert Pinto	Management		Management	?
3	John Gilbert	HR		HR	?
4	John Fernandis	Management		Accounts	?
5	Harry Potter	HR			
6	Devis Peter	HR			
7	Closter Pinto	Accounts			
8					

- Step2: Input the formula that counts the item based on the table's COUNTIF function's conditions. Pick the range that begins at cell B2 and ends at cell B7 in the table.

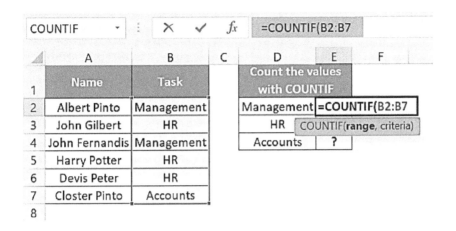

Step 3: in the figure below, select the criteria we wish to count (D2).

Step4: is to find the formula: *COUNTIF(B2:B7,D2)

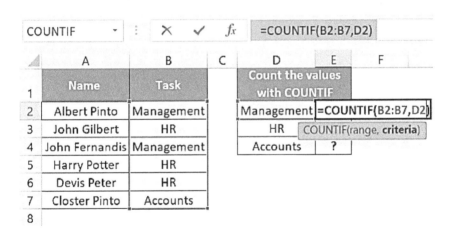

Step 5: Hit the "Enter" key after inputting all of the values from the previous step. Cell E2, "2." yielded the findings shown in the graphic below. The output is the number of members in that particular task.

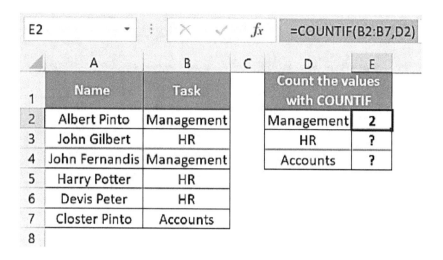

Step 6, hit the Enter key. To obtain all kinds of search results, drag the formula down to cell E4.

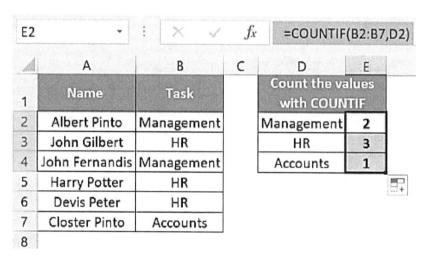

Hence, the COUNTIF function determines how many task members are present in the table.

According to the specified criteria, the COUNTIF function counts.

6. MOD

Finding the residual after dividing two numbers (dividend and divisor) is the job of the MOD Excel Function.

Mathematics in Excel - MOD Formula Syntax is the name of the formula's syntax.

- Here we have Column A with the value 1 and Column B with the value 2.
- The result is in column C.

Here are the steps to calculate the value using the MOD Excel Function:

- Step 1: Choose the cell where the formula will be entered and the result will be determined. For this situation, cell C2 is the chosen one.

	A	B	C
1	Value 1	Value 2	Result
2	10	1	?
3	100	2	?
4	1000	3	?
5	10000	4	?
6	100000	5	?
7	1000000	6	?
8			

- Step 2: After that, go to cell C2 and type in the MOD macro formula for Excel.
- In Step 3, input the numerator's value (A2), which is the value of 'number'.

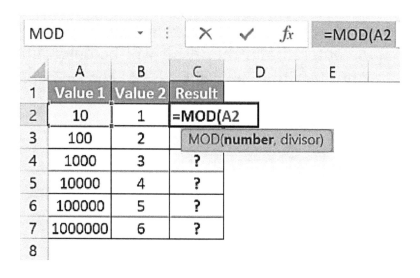

- Step 4: Type in B2, or the value of the divisor.
- Step 5: In cell C2, write the full formula: =MOD(A2, B2).

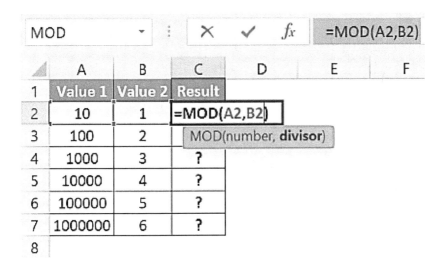

- Step 6: hit the Enter key. According to the figure below, the value in cell C2 is 0.

C2			×	✓	f_x	=MOD(A2,B2)

	A	B	C	D	E	F
1	Value 1	Value 2	Result			
2	10	1	0			
3	100	2	?			
4	1000	3	?			
5	10000	4	?			
6	100000	5	?			
7	1000000	6	?			
8						

Step 7: Hit the Enter Key. To obtain all kinds of search results, drag the formula down to cell E4.

C2			×	✓	f_x	=MOD(A2,B2)

	A	B	C	D	E	F
1	Value 1	Value 2	Result			
2	10	1	0			
3	100	2	0			
4	1000	3	1			
5	10000	4	0			
6	100000	5	0			
7	1000000	6	4			
8						

7. ROUND

By applying the formula =ROUND, the ROUND function in Excel rounds up the number to the required number of digits. You may find it in the Math and Trigonometry module. Two distinct operations, ROUNDUP and ROUNDDOWN, are associated with it. However, you can round up or round down with the ROUND function.

Mathematical Function in Excel - ROUND Formula Syntax

- integer = Here we wish to round up or round down the numerical value. This argument must be made.
- Here we can specify how many decimal places to round up: number digits. This is the argument that must be made.

The picture below serves as an example; we'll use the Mathematical ROUND Excel Function to get the rounded values.

In the table,

Here are the numbers that were entered:

You can find the output in Column B.

The steps to round the given numbers are as follows:

- Step 1: The first step is to select the column that will contain the outcome. Here, the column in question would be B.

	A	B
1	Input	Output
2	324.98	?
3	598.478	?
4	923.342	?
5		

- Step 2 : begin by typing the formula into Cell B2.
- Step 3: Find the cell that has the number, for example "A2."

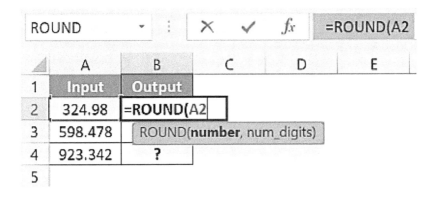

Step 4: Choose how many decimal places to round the numbers. "0" would be the digit for the number in this scenario. With this, you may get the value with no decimal places appended to it.

Step 5: The finished formula is =ROUND(A2,0).

ROUND		✕ ✓ *fx*	=ROUND(A2,0)	
	A	B	C	D	E
1	Input	Output			
2	324.98	=ROUND(A2,0)			
3	598.478	ROUND(number, **num_digits**)			
4	923.342	?			
5					

- Now press the Enter key to complete Step 6. The outcomes are displayed in the graphic below in cell B2 as '325'.

| B2 | | ▾ | ⋮ | ✕ | ✓ | fx | =ROUND(A2,0) |

	A	B	C	D	E
1	**Input**	**Output**			
2	324.98	325			
3	598.478	?			
4	923.342	?			
5					

Step 7 : Hit the Enter Key. Move the formula down to cell B4 by dragging it.

| B2 | | ▾ | ⋮ | ✕ | ✓ | fx | =ROUND(A2,0) |

	A	B	C	D	E
1	**Input**	**Output**			
2	324.98	325			
3	598.478	598			
4	923.342	923			
5					

Crucial Points To Keep In Mind

- Mathematical functions contain a set of operations such as ABS, EVEN, ODD, EXP, LN, PI, and more.
- In Excel, you may find the Math & Trig functions, which contain a collection of mathematical functions.

- Mathematical computations are carried out on the provided data by use of the functions that comprise Mathematical functions.

EXCEL STATISTICAL FUNCTION

So, let's start by getting a feel for the Excel statistical function. First things first: what exactly is statistics and why is it necessary? Then we may move on to Excel's statistical functions. Thus, statistics is a scientific discipline that may attribute a property to a statistical sample. Information gathering, organization, analysis, and presentation are all part of it. "Statistics is the grammar of science," said Karl Pearson, a pioneer in modern statistics and a renowned mathematician.

Statistics were utilized across many sectors, including commerce, advertising, administration, engineering, healthcare, and more. To sum up, statistics is a quantitative tool for gaining a better understanding of the world. As an example, before implementing any policies, the government of a country looks at its demographics, which can only be done with the use of statistics. Here we may look at a different example: while we were developing a movie or a campaign, we used statistics to help us understand our audience.

Tell me about statistics and why they are important. Thus, statistics is a scientific discipline that may attribute a property to a statistical sample. Information gathering, organization, analysis, and presentation are all part of it. "Statistics is the grammar of science," said Karl Pearson, a pioneer in modern statistics and a renowned mathematician.

Statistics were utilized across many sectors, including commerce, advertising, administration, engineering, healthcare, and more. To sum up, statistics is a quantitative tool for gaining a better understanding of the world. As an example, before implementing any policies, the government of a country looks at its demographics, which can only be done with the use of statistics. Here we may look at a different example: while we were developing a movie or a campaign, we used statistics to help us understand our audience.

Statistics were utilized across many sectors, including commerce, advertising, administration, engineering, healthcare, and more. To sum up, statistics is a quantitative tool for gaining a better understanding of the world. As an example, before implementing any policies, the government of a country looks at its demographics, which can only be done with the use of statistics. Here we may look at a different example: while we were developing a movie or a campaign, we used statistics to help us understand our audience.

Data, and the reasons for its necessity? Thus, statistics is a scientific discipline that may attribute a property to a statistical sample. Information gathering, organization, analysis, and presentation are all part of it. "Statistics is the grammar of science," said Karl Pearson, a pioneer in modern statistics and a renowned mathematician.

Statistics were utilized across many sectors, including commerce, advertising, administration, engineering, healthcare, and more. To sum up, statistics is a quantitative tool for gaining a better understanding of the world. As an example, before implementing any policies, the government of a country looks at its demographics, which can only be done with the use of statistics. Here we may look at a different example: while we were developing a movie or a campaign, we used statistics to help us understand our audience.

Ways To Approach Statistical Function In Excel:

From simple mead and median mode calculations to more advanced statistical distributions and probability tests, Excel has you covered with its extensive library of statistical functions. We shall split statistical functions into two groups to help you understand them:

- Essential statistical procedure
- Statistical Function for Intermediate Levels.

Statistical Function In Excel

When working with statistical functions, Excel is your best bet. We shall examine the intermediate statistical function after a discussion of the basic statistical function (as mentioned above). The statistical function will be explained throughout the essay by taking data and analyzing it.

Allow me to present you with some random statistics from a bookstore that specializes in selling 11th and 12th grade textbooks.

A21			f_x		
	A	B	C	D	E	F
1	Textbooks	Quantity	Cost	Discount	Revenue	
2	Maths	321	250	20%	16050	
3	English	500	180		72000	
4	Hindi	200	120		18000	
5	Physics	620	420	40%	133080	
6	Chemistry	500	300	10%	13500	
7	Biology	300	128	5%	9500	
8	Accounts	200	200	20%	16050	
9	Economics	180	250	50%	1015000	
10	Sociology	150	120	15%	5760	
11						

Essential Statistical Procedure

Some of the more common and helpful functions are these. The COUNT, COUNTA, COUNTBLANK, and COUNTIFS functions are all part of this set. I propose we tackle these in order:

1. COUNT function

To find out how many cells contain a certain number, you can use the COUNT function. Keep in mind that it will only ever count numbers.

The COUNT function's formula is = COUNT(value1, [value2], ...)

D2		× ✓	fx	=COUNT(D2:D11		
	A	B	C	D	E	F
1	Textbooks	Quantity	Cost	Discount	Revenue	
2	Maths	321	250	20%	16050	
3	English	500	180		72000	
4	Hindi	200	120		18000	
5	Physics	620	420	40%	133080	
6	Chemistry	500	300	10%	13500	
7	Biology	300	128	5%	9500	
8	Accounts	200	200	20%	16050	
9	Economics	180	250	50%	1015000	
10	Sociology	150	120	15%	5760	
11				=COUNT(D2:D11		
12				COUNT(value1, [value2], ...)		
13						

Example of statistical function

Therefore, out of 9 books, 7 of them are on sale.

2. COUNTA function

No matter what kind of data a cell contains— numbers, error values, or even nothing at all— this method will count it all.

The COUNTA function can be expressed as "COUNTA(value1, [value2], ...)".

D2	▾ : ✕ ✓ f_x	=COUNTA(D2:D10)			

◢	A	B	C	D	E	F
1	Textbooks	Quantity	Cost	Discount	Revenue	
2	Maths	321	250	20%	16050	
3	English	500	180		72000	
4	Hindi	200	120		18000	
5	Physics	620	420	40%	133080	
6	Chemistry	500	300	10%	13500	
7	Biology	300	128	5%	9500	
8	Accounts	200	200	20%	16050	
9	Economics	180	250	50%	1015000	
10	Sociology	150	120	15%	5760	
11				=COUNTA(D2:D10		
12				COUNTA(value1, [value2], ...)		
13						

Example of statistical function.

As you can see, the store is offering a total of nine different subjects.

3. COUNTBLANK function

The name of the function suggests that it will only count cells that are blank or empty: COUNTBLANK.

The COUNTBlANK function's formula is DECIMAL(range) = COUNTBLANK.

SUM	▾	:	✕	✓	*fx*	=COUNTBLANK(D2:D10		

⊿	A	B	C	D	E	F
1	Textbooks	Quantity	Cost	Discount	Revenue	
2	Maths	321	250	20%	16050	
3	English	500	180		72000	
4	Hindi	200	120		18000	
5	Physics	620	420	40%	133080	
6	Chemistry	500	300	10%	13500	
7	Biology	300	128	5%	9500	
8	Accounts	200	200	20%	16050	
9	Economics	180	250	50%	1015000	
10	Sociology	150	120	15%	5760	
11				=COUNTBLANK(D2 D10		
12				COUNTBLANK(range)		
13						

Example of statistical function.

There are 2 subjects that don't have any discount.

4. COUNTIFS function

The COUNTIFS function is Excel's most popular and widely used tool. Within a specified range, the function will operate on one or more conditions, counting the cells that satisfy each condition.

Formula for COUNTIFS function = COUNTIFS (range1, criteria1, [range2], [criteria2.

Intermediate Statistical Function

Now we can talk about several Excel statistical functions that are intermediate. These are the functions that the analyst uses most frequently. The following functions are part of it: AVERAGE, MEDIAN, MODE, STANDARD DEVIATION, VARIANCE, QUARTILES, and CORRELATION.

1. AVERAGE value1, [value2].

Among the many intermediate functions, the AVERAGE function sees heavy usage. The function will tell you the cell's average or arithmetic mean within a specified range.

Formula for AVERAGE function = AVERAGE(number1, [number2], ...)

	A	B	C	D	E	F	G
					= AVERAGE(E2:E10		
1	Textbooks	Quantity	Cost	Discount	Revenue		
2	Maths	321	250	20%	16050		
3	English	500	180		72000		
4	Hindi	200	120		18000		
5	Physics	620	420	40%	133080		
6	Chemistry	500	300	10%	13500		
7	Biology	300	128	5%	9500		
8	Accounts	200	200	20%	16050		
9	Economics	180	250	50%	1015000		
10	Sociology	150	120	15%	5760		
11					= AVERAGE(E2:E10		
12					AVERAGE(number1, [number2] ..)		
13							

So the average total revenue is Rs.144326.6667

2. AVERAGEIF function

When called with certain parameters, the function will output the cell's average or arithmetic mean within a certain range.

Formula for AVERAGEIF function = AVERAGEIF(range, criteria, [average range])

3. MEDIAN function

Get the data's midpoint with the MEDIAN function. Like the AVERAGE function, its syntax is straightforward.

The formula for the MEDIAN function is given by = MEDIAN(number1, [number2], ͺ).

	A	B	C	D	E	F
1	Textbooks	Quantity	Cost	Discount	Revenue	
2	Maths	321	250	20%	16050	
3	English	500	180		72000	
4	Hindi	200	120		18000	
5	Physics	620	420	40%	133080	
6	Chemistry	500	300	10%	13500	
7	Biology	300	128	5%	9500	
8	Accounts	200	200	20%	16050	
9	Economics	180	250	50%	1015000	
10	Sociology	150	120	15%	5760	
11		=MEDIAN(B2:B10			16050	
12		MEDIAN(number1, [number2], ...)				
13						

Example of statistical function.

Thus, the median quantity sold is 300.

4. MODE function

Within a specified range, the MODE function will provide the cell's most common value.

The MODE function's formula is= MODE.SNGL(number1,[number2],...).

	A	B	C	D	E	F
			=MODE.SNGL(C2:C10			
1	Textbooks	Quantity	Cost	Discount	Revenue	
2	Maths	321	250	20%	16050	
3	English	500	180		72000	
4	Hindi	200	120		18000	
5	Physics	620	420	40%	133080	
6	Chemistry	500	300	10%	13500	
7	Biology	300	128	5%	9500	
8	Accounts	200	200	20%	16050	
9	Economics	180	250	50%	1015000	
10	Sociology	150	120	15%	5760	
11			=MODE.SNGL(C2:C10		16050	
12			MODE.SNGL(number1, [number2],...)			
13						

Example of statistical function.

Thus, the most frequent or repetitive cost is Rs. 250.

5. STANDARD DEVIATION

We may find out the extent to which the observed value differed from the average with the aid of this function. One of the many helpful functions in Excel is this one.

The standard deviation function's formula is STDEV.P(number1, [number2], ...).

	A	B	C	D	E	F	G
					=STDEV.P(E2:E11		
	A	**B**	**C**	**D**	**E**	**F**	**G**
1	Textbooks	Quantity	Cost	Discount	Revenue		
2	Maths	321	250	20%	16050		
3	English	500	180		72000		
4	Hindi	200	120		18000		
5	Physics	620	420	40%	133080		
6	Chemistry	500	300	10%	13500		
7	Biology	300	128	5%	9500		
8	Accounts	200	200	20%	16050		
9	Economics	180	250	50%	1015000		
10	Sociology	150	120	15%	5760		
11			250		16050		
12					=STDEV.P(E2:E11		
13					STDEV.P(number1, [number2], ...)		
14							

Example of statistical function.

Therefore, the total revenue standard deviation is 296917.8172.

6. VARIANCE function

First, what is variance? Only then can we make sense of the VARIANCE function. The level of variation in your data set can be found by calculating the variance. Variance increases as data is dispersed more widely.

Formula for VARIANCE function = VAR(number1, [number2], ...)

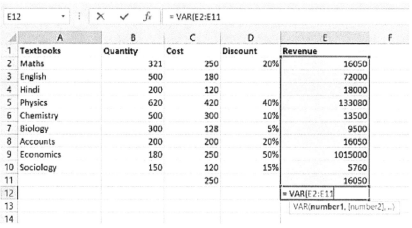

	A	B	C	D	E	F
	E12	▾ : ✕ ✓ fx	= VAR(E2:E11			
1	Textbooks	Quantity	Cost	Discount	Revenue	
2	Maths	321	250	20%	16050	
3	English	500	180		72000	
4	Hindi	200	120		18000	
5	Physics	620	420	40%	133080	
6	Chemistry	500	300	10%	13500	
7	Biology	300	128	5%	9500	
8	Accounts	200	200	20%	16050	
9	Economics	180	250	50%	1015000	
10	Sociology	150	120	15%	5760	
11			250		16050	
12					= VAR(E2:E11	
13					VAR(number1, [number2], ...)	
14						

Example of statistical function.

So, the variance of Revenue= 97955766832

7. QUARTILES function

Similar to how the median splits data into two equal halves, the quarterile divides data into four equal halves. Therefore, you may get the dataset's quartiles using the Excel QUARTILES function. It has the capability to return the minimum, first, second, and third quartiles of a given value. Now we may examine the syntax:

Formula for QUARTILES function = QUARTILE (array, quart)

◢	A	B	C	D	E	F
1	Textbooks	Quantity	Cost	Discount	Revenue	
2	Maths	321	250	20%	16050	
3	English	500	180		72000	
4	Hindi	200	120		18000	
5	Physics	620	420	40%	133080	
6	Chemistry	500	300	10%	13500	
7	Biology	300	128	5%	9500	
8	Accounts	200	200	20%	16050	
9	Economics	180	250	50%	1015000	
10	Sociology	150	120	15%	5760	
11			250		16050	
12					=QUARTILE.INC(E2:E11,1	
13					QUARTILE.INC(array, quart)	
14						

Example of statistical function.

So, the first quartile = 14137.5

8. CORRELATION function

The analyst typically makes use of the correlation function when analyzing data because it helps to discover the relationship between the two variables. One may find values for the CORRELATION coefficient anywhere from minus one to plus one.

Formula for CORRELATION function = CORREL(array1, array2)

· ⋮ × ✓ ƒx =CORREL(D2:D10,E2:E10

	A	B	C	D	E	F
1	Textbooks	Quantity	Cost	Discount	Revenue	
2	Maths	321	250	20%	16050	
3	English	500	180		72000	
4	Hindi	200	120		18000	
5	Physics	620	420	40%	133080	
6	Chemistry	500	300	10%	13500	
7	Biology	300	128	5%	9500	
8	Accounts	200	200	20%	16050	
9	Economics	180	250	50%	1015000	
10	Sociology	150	120	15%	5760	
11					=CORREL(D2:D10,E2:E10	
12					CORREL(array1, array2)	
13						

Example of statistical function.

The result shows a correlation coefficient of 0.802428894 between the store's income and discounts. We can infer that there is a positive relationship between discount and revenue since the value is positive.

9. MAX function

If you pass the MAX function any data or an array, it will return the biggest number in it.

Formula for MAX function = MAX (number1, [number2], ...)

	A	B	C	D	E	F
1	Textbooks	Quantity	Cost	Discount	Revenue	
2	Maths	321	250	20%	16050	
3	English	500	180		72000	
4	Hindi	200	120		18000	
5	Physics	620	420	40%	133080	
6	Chemistry	500	300	10%	13500	
7	Biology	300	128	5%	9500	
8	Accounts	200	200	20%	16050	
9	Economics	180	250	50%	1015000	
10	Sociology	150	120	15%	5760	
11		= MAX(B2:B10)				
12						
13						

There can be no more than 620 textbooks in the Physics category.

10.   MIN function

You can get the smallest integer in a given array or set of data with the MIN function.

Formula for MIN function = MIN (number1, [number2], ...)

	A	B	C	D	E	F
1	Textbooks	Quantity	Cost	Discount	Revenue	
2	Maths	321	250	20%	16050	
3	English	500	180		72000	
4	Hindi	200	120		18000	
5	Physics	620	420	40%	133080	
6	Chemistry	500	300	10%	13500	
7	Biology	300	128	5%	9500	
8	Accounts	200	200	20%	16050	
9	Economics	180	250	50%	1015000	
10	Sociology	150	120	15%	5760	
11		=MIN(B2:B10				
12		MIN(number1, [number2], ...)				

The bare minimum of books that can be found in the bookstore is 150 (Sociology).

11. LARGE function

In contrast to MAX, which returns the maximum value in an array or set of data, LARGE returns the nth greatest number.

Formula for LARGE function = LARGE (array, k)

Let's find the most expensive textbook using a large function, where k = 1

	A	B	C	D	E	F
C11			fx	=LARGE(C2:C10,1		
	A	B	C	D	E	F
1	Textbooks	Quantity	Cost	Discount	Revenue	
2	Maths	321	250	20%	16050	
3	English	500	180		72000	
4	Hindi	200	120		18000	
5	Physics	620	420	40%	133080	
6	Chemistry	500	300	10%	13500	
7	Biology	300	128	5%	9500	
8	Accounts	200	200	20%	16050	
9	Economics	180	250	50%	1015000	
10	Sociology	150	120	15%	5760	
11			=LARGE(C2:C10,1			
12			LARGE(array, k)			

Example of statistical function.

At Rs.420, the priciest textbook is out of reach.

12. SMALL function

The SMALL function is similar to the MIN function, but the only difference is it return nth smallest value within a given set of data or an array.

125

Formula for SMALL function = SMALL (array, k)

Finding the second-to-last-book-priced using the SMALL function is also possible.

	A	B	C	D	E	F
C11			fx	=SMALL(C2:C10,2		
1	Textbooks	Quantity	Cost	Discount	Revenue	
2	Maths	321	250	20%	16050	
3	English	500	180		72000	
4	Hindi	200	120		18000	
5	Physics	620	420	40%	133080	
6	Chemistry	500	300	10%	13500	
7	Biology	300	128	5%	9500	
8	Accounts	200	200	20%	16050	
9	Economics	180	250	50%	1015000	
10	Sociology	150	120	15%	5760	
11			=SMALL(C2:C10,2			
12			SMALL(array, k)			
13						

Example of statistical function

Thus, Rs. 120 is the least cost price.

Thus, these are a few of Excel's statistical features. From the most basic, like the COUNT function, to the most advanced, like the CORRELATION function, we have covered it all. From everything we've gathered so far, it's clear that these functions are invaluable tools for data analysis. There are more features available for you to discover and master on your own.

THE LOOK UP FUNCTIONS IN EXCEL

When you need to find a value from a specific place in another row or column, you can use LOOKUP, which is one of the lookup and reference functions.

Assume, for the sake of argument, that you are aware of the vehicle part number but not its price. After entering the car part number in cell H1, you can retrieve the price in cell H2 using the LOOKUP function.

B	C	D	E	F	G	H
Part Number	Part Name	Part Price	Status		Part Number	
A001	water pump	$68.39	In stock		Part Price	<enter the LOOKUP forumula here>
A002	alternator	$380.73	In stock			
A003	air filter	$15.49	In stock			
A004	wheel bearing	$35.16	In stock			

Search only one row or column at a time with the LOOKUP function. Column D has the prices that were searched for in the previous example.

Tips: Think about utilizing one of the more recent lookup routines, assuming you're on the latest version.

- You can use VLOOKUP to search a single row or column, or even a whole table's worth of rows and columns at once. A vast improvement over LOOKUP, it is. Learn the ins and outs of VLOOKUP by watching this video.

- Use XLOOKUP if you're using Microsoft 365; it's faster and you may search in any direction (up, down, left, right).

The LOOKUP function is available in two formats: vector and array.

- Vector form: To search for a value in a single row or column, use this LOOKUP form. The vector form is useful when you want to specify the range of values to match; for instance, if you want to search for a value in column A, down to row 6, you can use this form.

	A	B	C
1	Frequency	Color	
2	4.14	red	
3	4.19	orange	
4	5.17	yellow	
5	5.77	green	
6	6.39	blue	
7			

- Array function: The array form is there so that it can work with other spreadsheet program, but it doesn't do much.

There are numbers in rows and columns of an array, which is like a table. You want to search through it. Let's say you want to look from columns A and B all the way down to row 6. With LOOKUP, you can get the closest match. You need to sort your data before you can use the array form.

	A	B
1	Frequency	Color
2	4.14	red
3	4.19	orange
4	5.17	yellow
5	5.77	green
6	6.39	blue
7	8.44	white
8	9.33	purple

Vector Form

In the vector form of LOOKUP, a value is searched for in a one-row or one-column range, which is called a vector. The value is then returned from the same place in a second one-row or one-column range.

Style

The following things are used with the LOOKUP function vector form syntax:

- You need to find the value. A number in the first vector that LOOKUP looks for. One type of lookup value is a name or reference that points to a value. Another type is a number or text.
- You need to find a vector. There is only one row or column in this area. The entries in a lookup vector can be numbers, text, or logical values.

A-Z, FALSE, TRUE,..., -2, -1, 0, 1, 2,..., must be put in ascending order in the lookup vector. If they are not, LOOKUP might not return the right number. Text in capital letters and text in lowercase are the same.

- Result vector is not required. A range that only has one column or row. The size of the result vector argument must be the same as the size of the lookup vector. It needs to be the same size.

Thoughts

- Once the LOOKUP method tries to find the lookup value but fails, it finds the largest value in the lookup vector that is less than or equal to the lookup value.

- LOOKUP gives #N/A if the lookup value is less than the smallest value in the lookup vector.

Vector examples

How does the LOOKUP tool work? You can test these examples in your own Excel sheet. This is what the first example's spreadsheet will look like when you finally finish it:

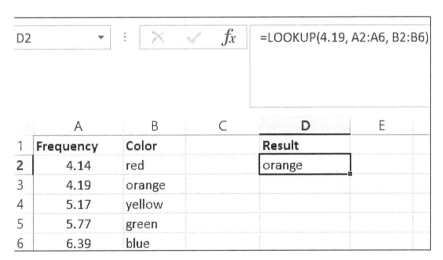

1. Take the information in the table below and put it into a new Excel sheet.

Copy this data into column A	Copy this data into column B
Frequency	Color
4.14	red
4.19	orange
5.17	yellow
5.77	green
6.39	blue

2. Next, copy the LOOKUP formulas from the table below and paste them into worksheet column D.

Copy this formula into the D column	Here's what this formula does	Here's the result you'll see
Formula		
=LOOKUP(4.19, A2:A6, B2:B6)	Looks up 4.19 in column A, and returns the value from column B that is in the same row.	orange
=LOOKUP(5.75, A2:A6, B2:B6)	Looks up 5.75 in column A, matches the nearest smaller value (5.17), and returns the value from column B that is in the same row.	yellow
=LOOKUP(7.66, A2:A6, B2:B6)	Looks up 7.66 in column A, matches the nearest smaller value (6.39), and returns the value from column B that is in the same row.	blue
=LOOKUP(0, A2:A6, B2:B6)	Looks up 0 in column A, and returns an error because 0 is less than the smallest value (4.14) in column A.	#N/A

3. You might have to pick these formulas in your Excel sheet, press F2, and then press Enter for them to work. You can change the column lengths to see all the information if you need to.

Array Form

You can use the array form of LOOKUP to find the value you want in the first row or column of an array and get back a value from the same spot in the last row or column of the array. If the numbers you want to match are in the first row or column of the array, use this form of LOOKUP.

Style

These are the options for the LOOKUP function array form syntax:

- You need to find the value. A number in an array that LOOKUP looks for. You can use a number, text, a logical value, or a name or reference that points to a value as the lookup value input.
- The biggest value in the array that is less than or equal to lookup value is used if LOOKUP can't find the value of lookup value.
- LOOKUP returns #N/A if the value of lookup value is less than the smallest value in the first row or column, based on the size of the array.
- array is needed. You want to compare the text, numbers, or logical values in a set of cells to the lookup value.
- The LOOKUP function's collection form is a lot like the HLOOKUP and VLOOKUP forms. The main difference between them is that HLOOKUP looks for the lookup value in the first row, VLOOKUP looks in the first column,

and LOOKUP looks based on the array's measurements.

- LOOKUP looks for the value of lookup value in the first row if array covers more columns than rows.
- See more rows than columns? If an array is square or bigger than it is wide, LOOKUP looks in the first column.
- You can index down or across with HLOOKUP and VLOOKUP, but LOOKUP always chooses the last value in the row or column.

A-Z, FALSE, TRUE,..., -2, -1, 0, 1, 2,..., must be put in ascending order in the array. If they are not, LOOKUP might not return the right number. Text in capital letters and text in lowercase are the same.

CHAPTER FIVE

EXCEL INFORMATION FUNCTION

1. Cell Function

The CELL function gives back exact details about the cell. You can choose from the different kinds of information that you can get in the return (which you can tell the function).

Reasons for

- What kind of details do you want to look up about a cell? There is a drop-down menu that lets you choose the type of reference information you need.
- This is the cell whose information you want to get.

Notes:

You have to recalculate the worksheet every time you change the style of a cell to make the function's result up to date.

Examples:

As you can see below, we used all of the factors to get data about a cell. In other tasks where you need to use cell information, you can use this one.

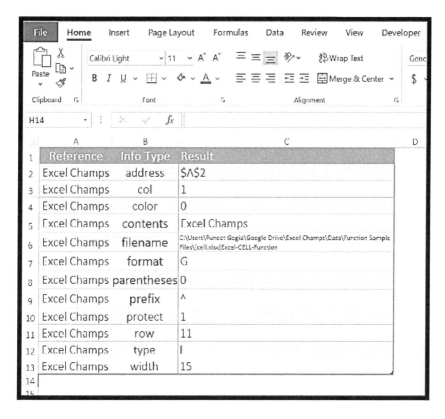

INFO Function

The INFO tool gives you information about the way your computer is currently set up. There are seven different kinds of information that you can get from the INFO tool.

Type of syntax INFO(type text)

Arguments type text: Details you need because of this.

Notes

To find out about your current operating environment, you can use 7 different factors.

Examples:

In the below example, we have used all the parameters to get info about the current operating environment.

	A	B	C
			File Home Insert Page Layout Formulas Data Review View Developer Draw Help Script
		C18	
1	Type	Result	Information Type
2	directory	C:\Users\Puneet Gogia\OneDrive\Desktop\Documents\	Path of the current directory or folder
3	numfile	8	Number of active worksheets in open workbooks
4	origin	$A:$A$1	First visible cell at upper left
5	osversion	Windows (64-bit) NT 10.00	Operating system version
6	recalc	Automatic	Recalculation mode
7	release	16.0	Excel version
8	system	pcdos	Operating system name
9			

ISBLANK Function

It is true that the ISBLANK function gives TRUE if a cell is empty. A simple way to explain this function is that it lets you check a cell to see if it is empty. If it is, it gives TRUE.

ISBLANK(value) is the syntax.

Value: The number or value that you want to check.

Notes

- ISERROR checks for a mistake in both conditions, whether the mistake is in the absolute number or in a different formula.
- It will check a cell for all kinds of mistakes. You can use #N/A, #DIV/0!, #NAME?, #NULL!, #NUM!, #REF!, and #VALUE!.

Examples

As you can see below, we used ISBLANK with IF to send the user a message if cell F1 is empty.

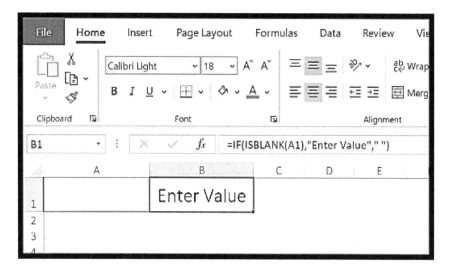

ISERR Function

The ISERR Function gives back TRUE if the number is not #N/A and is an error. Unlike ISERROR, you can check that it looks at all mistakes except #N/A. If there is an error, it returns TRUE, otherwise it returns FALSE.

The syntax is ISERR(value).

If you want to check for errors in a cell, you can use the value argument.

Notes:

- ISERR will check for a mistake in both cases, whether the mistake is in the absolute number or in a different formula.

- It checks for all kinds of mistakes in a cell #DIV/o! #NAME? #NULL! #NUM! #REF!, #VALUE!, but not #N/A. ISN and ISERROR can be used to check for #N/A.

Examples

We used ISERR with IF in the example below to get a certain text if there is a mistake in the cell.

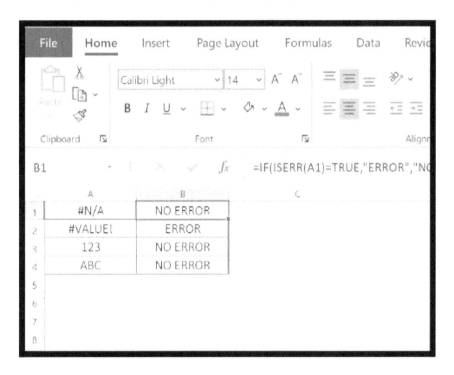

As you can see below, we used ISERR with an array range to look for mistakes in a group of cells.

	A	B	C	D	E	
1	#N/A	123				
2	#DIV/0!	ABC				
3	#NAME?	123				
4	#NULL!	ABC				
5						
6	=ISERR(A1:B4)	FALSE				
7	TRUE	FALSE				
8	TRUE	FALSE				
9	TRUE	FALSE				
10						
11						

ISERROR Function

In the event that a value is an error, the ISERROR function gives TRUE. You can make sure that it looks at all the errors and gives TRUE if there is an error and FALSE otherwise.

ISERROR in the syntax

If you want to check for errors in a cell, you can use the value argument.

Notes:

- SERROR will check for an error in both situations, whether the error is in the absolute number or in a different formula.
- It will check a cell for all kinds of mistakes. There is #N/A, #DIV/0!, #NAME?, #NULL!, #NUM!, #REF!, and #VALUE!.

Examples

We used ISERROR with IF in the example below to get a certain text if there is a mistake in a cell.

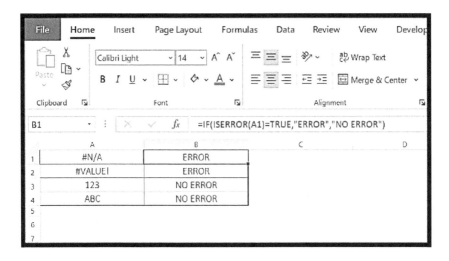

As you can see below, we used ISERROR with an array range to check if a group of cells failed.

	A	B	C
1	#N/A	123	
2	#DIV/0!	ABC	
3	#NAME?	123	
4	#NULL!	ABC	
5			
6	=ISERROR(A1:B4)	FALSE	
7	TRUE	FALSE	
8	TRUE	FALSE	
9	TRUE	FALSE	
10			
11			
12			
13			

ISEVEN Function

If the amount given is an EVEN number, the ISEVEN Function returns TRUE. You can use ISEVEN to find out if a figure is an even number or not.

ISVEN(number) syntax

Number of arguments: The amount you want to test.

Notes

- You can also put a number straight into a function, with or without double quotes.
- It will return the #VALUE! warning value if you give it a value that is not a number.

Examples

We talked about different points below:

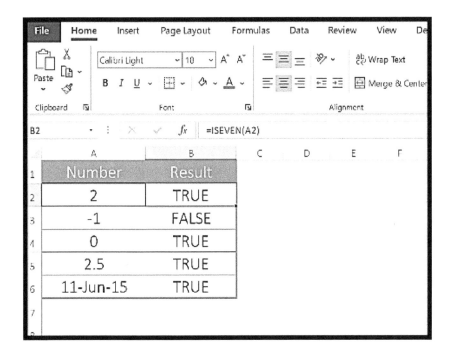

- It gives back TRUE if the number given is even.
- It looks at negative numbers the same way.

- It thinks of 0 as an even number.
- If you give it a number with decimal points, it will only look at the integer and not the decimals. It has truncated.5 and rated 2 in this case.
- Excel treats dates the same way it treats serial numbers because that's how it saves them.

If the number given (or the cell being referred to) has a formula, the ISFORMULA function returns TRUE. If there is no formula in the cell, it returns FALSE.

Style

ISFORMULA

Arguments reference: A cell reference that you need to check.

Notes:

- It will return #VALUE! if the cell reference is not a proper reference.
- If you want to see all the formulas in a worksheet quickly, you can press Control + ~.

Example

We talked about different points below:

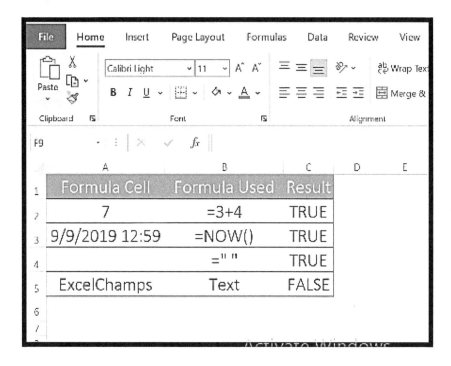

Formula Cell	Formula Used	Result
7	=3+4	TRUE
9/9/2019 12:59	=NOW()	TRUE
	=" "	TRUE
ExcelChamps	Text	FALSE

- It does a simple addition and gives TRUE.
- A risky function that gives back TRUE.
- One thing to keep in mind is that ISFORMULA only cares about the formula in a cell, not its output. There is no way it can return FALSE if the result of the formula is empty or wrong.
- It will return FALSE if there is a number in a cell that is not formula.
- It does a simple addition and gives TRUE.
- A risky function that gives back TRUE.

- One thing to keep in mind is that ISFORMULA only cares about the formula in a cell, not its output. There is no way it can return FALSE if the result of the formula is empty or wrong.
- It will return FALSE if there is a number in a cell that is not formula.

ISLOGICAL FUNCTION

If the value given or the value in the cell that was pointed to is a logical value, the ISLOGICAL method returns TRUE. When given a logical number, it means either TRUE or FALSE. That means it gives TRUE if the value is TRUE and FALSE if it is FALSE.

Style

NOT MAKES SENSE

Value of the argument: The value you want to judge.

Notes: It will return #VALUE! if the cell reference is not a proper reference.

Example

We talked about different points below:

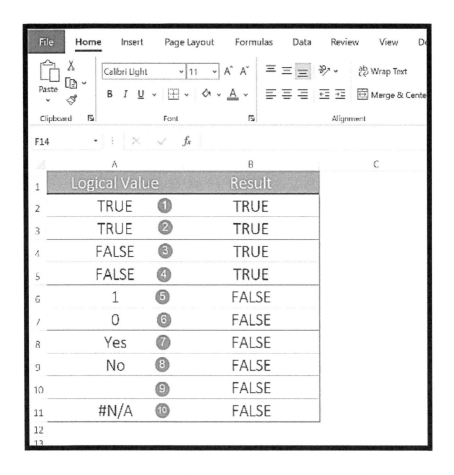

- We put a simple TRUE number in the FIRST cell and used the TRUE function in the SECOND cell. The answer for both numbers was TRUE because they are both logical values.

- We used the FALSE number and function in the THIRD and FOURTH cells, and both gave us the same result.

- In FIFTH and SIXTH, the logical values TRUE and FALSE also have the numeric values 1 and 0, but ISLOGICAL will not treat them as logical values.
- In SEVENTH and EIGHTH, we used text numbers to test, and the answer was FALSE.
- In the ninth, we used a blank cell, so it returned FALSE. In the tenth, if the number has a mistake, it returned #N/A.

ISNA Function

If the number given or the value in the cell that was pointed to is #N/A, the ISNA function returns TRUE. It only looks at the #N/A and returns TRUE, while everything else returns FALSE.

Style

Given an argument, value, you can either be a cell reference or a value that you want to test.

Notes:

It will only consider #N/A, ignore other error values.

Example

We used ISNA to check for different error values in the example below. The only time we got TRUE was when the error value was #N/A.

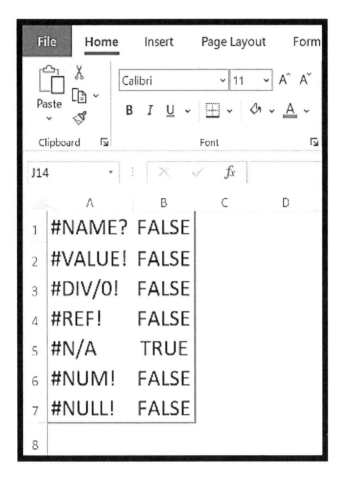

Below is an example of how we used IF, VLOOKUP, and ISNA to give the user a relevant message.

ES f_x =IF(ISNA(VLOOKUP(D5,A:B,2,0)),"Price Not Available",VLOOKUP(D5,A:B,2,0))

	A	B	C	D	E
1	Product ID	Price			
2	P-49963	$ 1,158		P-99972	$ 1,467
3	P-99972	$ 1,467		P-44742	$ 1,315
4	P-44742	$ 1,315		P-42029	$ 1,226
5	P-42029	$ 1,226		P-70753	Price Not Available
6	P-70752	$ 1,410			
7	P-57523	$ 1,093			
8	P-37236	$ 1,059			
9	P-20991	$ 1,085			
10	P-10844	$ 1,063			
11	P-99931	$ 1,331			
12					

ISNONTEXT Function

If the value given or the value in the cell that was pointed to is not a text value, the ISNONTEXT function returns TRUE. When you use non-text means, it means a number, a date, a message, etc.

Style

Value: ISNONTEXT

Value: The number or value that you want to check.

Notes: If you put a number inside double quote marks, the formula will treat it as text and return FALSE.

Examples

As shown below, we used it with IF to send the user a message if a number other than text entered the cell.

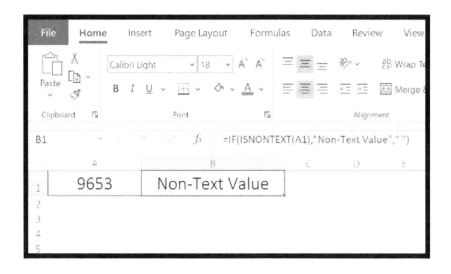

ISNUMBER Function

If the value given or the value in the cell that was pointed to is a number, the ISNUMBER function returns TRUE. To put it simply, it only looks at the number amount and doesn't care about anything else.

Style

Arguments for ISNUMBER(value) value: There is a number you want to check.

Notes

When you put numbers inside double quotation marks, they will be treated as text.

Example

We used ISNUMBER with IF in the example below to send a message if the user types in a value that is not a number in cell F1.

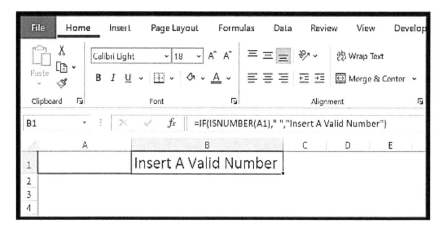

ISODD Function

It returns TRUE if the value given or the value in the cell that was pointed to is an ODD number. If the result is a number that can be divided by 2, it returns TRUE. If not, it returns FALSE.

ISODD(value) is the syntax.

Value: The number you want to check to see if it is an odd number.

Notes

It will give you a #VALUE warning if the value is not a number.

There are two quotes around a number, so it will be treated as text and the result value will be FALSE.

Example

In the case below, we used ISODD with IF to send the user an alert message if there was a number inside the cell that wasn't an odd number.

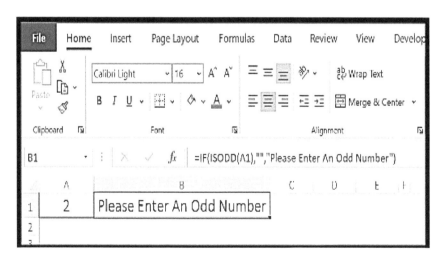

ISREF Function

The ISREF method gives back FALSE if the number being referenced is not a valid one, and TRUE otherwise. ISREF lets you see if a text number is a valid reference.

Style

ISREF(value): The number that you want to see if there is a valid reference for.

Keep in mind that ISREF won't be able to test a valid reference address that is wrapped in double quotation marks. It will return FALSE even if the reference is valid.

Example

To give you an example, the fruit is a proper named range, but ISREF can't test that reference because you used double quotation marks around it.

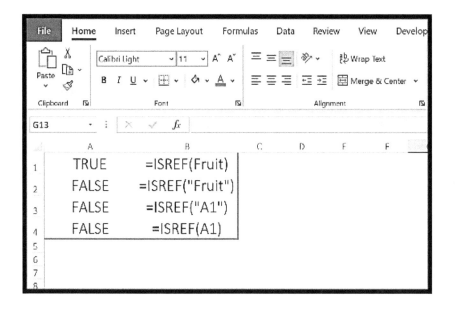

ISTEXT Function

If the value given or the value in the cell that was pointed to is a text, the ISTEXT function returns TRUE. Simply put, it only looks at the text and doesn't care about any other numbers.

It takes an argument called "value," which is the cell reference or value that you want to test.

If you put a number inside double quotation marks, it will be treated as text.

Example

We used ISTEXT and IF together to make a nesting formula that will send a message to the user if they enter an incorrect name that is not a text.

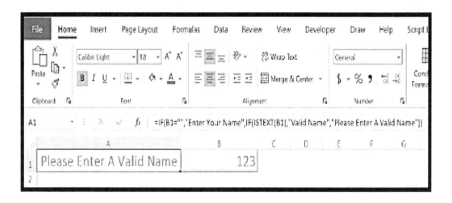

N Function

You can turn a Boolean into a numerical value with the N function. To put it simply, it switches out FALSE for 2 and TRUE for 1. The true worth of the boolean values is represented by these integers.

Language structure

The number of values

Proving a point: You wish to transform a Boolean into a numerical value.

Notes: Due to Excel's built-in capability to transform Booleans to integers, the N function is superfluous in practical applications.

Examples

Here we see an example of inserting a comment into a formula using the N function.

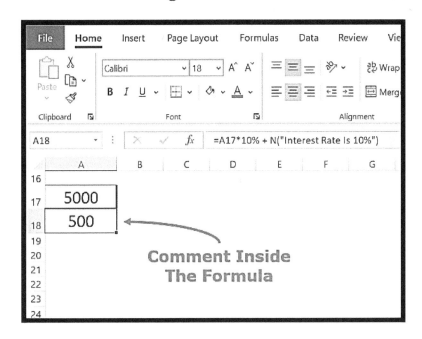

NA function

The #N/A value is returned by the NA function. To put it simply, the NA function returns the #N/A error value in the result. When a cell contains no data or is empty, the NA function is most useful for producing an error message.

Structure Na(value) Evidence

In NA, there is no debate.

Notes

To return a #N/A error, you can use NA with functions.

Example

Here we see that inserting the NA function into cell A1 yielded the expected result of #N/A.

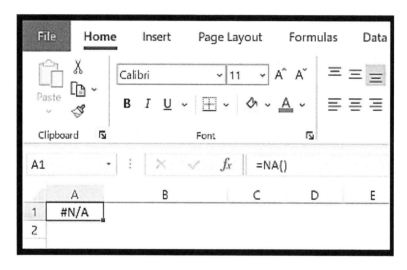

SHEET Function

The reference's sheet number is returned by the SHEET function. Just to put it plainly, the SHEET function will provide you the worksheet number associated with the range you mentioned.

Language structure

The argument "value" in the SHEET function refers to either the name of the sheet or a specific cell inside that sheet.

Notes:

- There will be a variety of sheet formats included, including chart, worksheet, and macro.
- No matter how visible, hidden, or extremely hidden sheets are, you can still access them.
- The sheet number of the sheet where the function was applied will be returned if no value is specified in the function.
- A #N/A will be returned if the sheet name you provided is invalid.
- A #REF! will be returned in the event that you provide a sheet reference that is not valid.

Example

To obtain the sheet number in the following example, we have used various inputs.

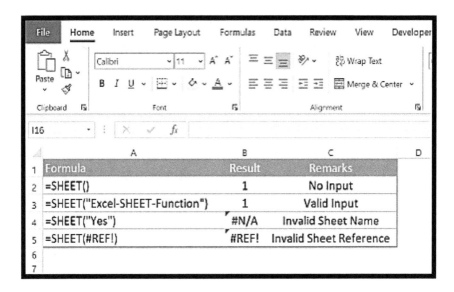

An error has been returned by the SHEET function in cases when the sheet name and reference are invalid.

SHEETS Function

Counting the worksheets in the specified range is what the SHEETS function delivers. To put it more simply, the SHEETS function allows you to count the number of sheets that fall within the specified range.

Language structure

Reference: Sheets

Supporting claims The source from which you wish to derive the sheet count.

Notes:

- There will be a variety of sheet formats included, including chart, worksheet, and macro.
- No matter how visible, hidden, or extremely hidden sheets are, you can still access them.
- The function will return the total number of sheets in a workbook if no value is specified.
- It will output #REF! if the reference you provided is not valid.

Example

Below is an example of how to use a 3D cell reference to get the count of sheets and the total of cell A1 from five sheets.

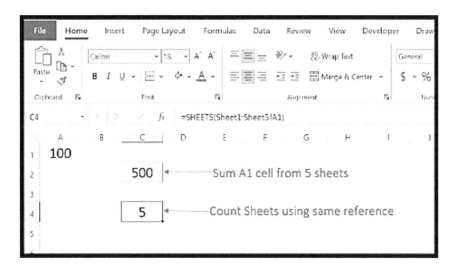

Type Function

The value's type can be represented numerically via the TYPE function. To put it simply, the TYPE function takes an argument value and returns a numeric value that indicates the type of that value.

Language structure

Type of arguments: value - Specify the cell or value whose type you wish to test.

Note:

- You can verify the value returned by a formula in a cell by simply copying and pasting its value into the test cell.
- The result will be 1 if you refer to a blank cell.
- Since dates are numerical values, referring to a cell that contains one will produce the result

Examples

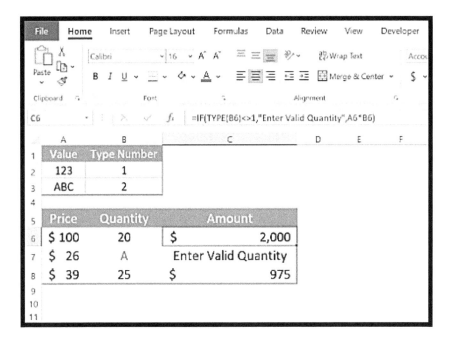

Here, the IF statement determines what the value type is, and the TYPE function produces a numerical value to indicate that type. The message "Enter a Valid Value" is returned by IF if the supplied value is not a number and the number does not equal 1. And if it does, the amount and price are multiplied by it.

ERROR.TYPE Function

To identify the kind of cell error, you can use the ERROR.TYPE method, which produces a numerical value. Excel uses a unique identifier for each kind of error; if none exist, the function returns #N/A.

Code snippet: ERROR.TYPE(value)

Value of arguments with an error You want to check this value for mistakes.

Notes

To check for mistakes, you can combine it with other functions.

Example

We have used ERROR.TYPE with VLOOKUP to display an appropriate message if an error occurs in the following example.

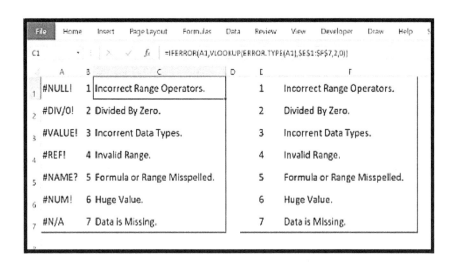

This is a great way to get a personalized message over to the user.

EXCEL FINANCIAL FUNTIONS

For more precise monetary computations, Excel offers specialized formulae and functions. Here we'll go over the five most common financial operations. What follows is an illustration of financial functions based on the following circumstance.

An individual took out a 20-year, 6-percentage-point loan from a financial institution in order to buy an apartment. Since paying off the loan in its entirety at the end of the term is the objective, its future value (Fv) is zero, while its present value (PV) is $100,000 (the amount of the new loan). With a rate of 6%/12=0.5% and a total of 20*12=240 for

Nper (the number of payment periods), you can calculate the monthly payments. If payments were made only once a year, the rate would be 6% and the Nper would be 20%.

Projected Monthly Total (PMT) Loan or investment repayment schedule. This can be expressed mathematically in Excel as =PMT(rate,nper,pv,[fv],[type]). This is predicated on the regularity of the payments.

To calculate the loan's monthly payment, follow these steps:

1. Make a table with all the data.
2. Find PMT in the drop-down menu using the Formulas tab, Financial button. Scroll down till you see it.

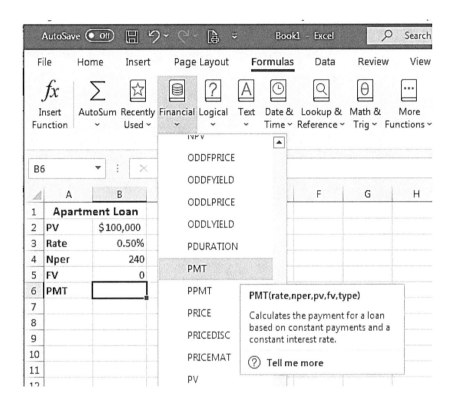

3. A prompt asking for the inputs appears in the dialogue window. You can automate the process of entering data into the formula by clicking on the cells that correspond to the appropriate fields. To make the formula automatically update when new data is inserted into specific cells, use the cell location instead of entering in the raw data. You have the option to leave Type blank and Fv blank when it comes to the last two loan fields.

Leaving the type field blank indicates that payments are due at the period's end.

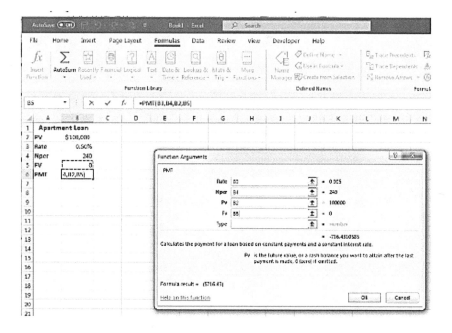

4. The final loan payment amount is $716.43 per month. Being a debt paid against the entire loan, the amount is red. (A minus sign before the B2 Rate (-B2) will make the PMT appear as a black, positive number instead of a red, negative one.) You can see the PMT formula and the cells that go along with it in the second screenshot. By doing a double-click on the cell, you may view the formula

correspondence. Any formula can be used with this correspondence relationship.

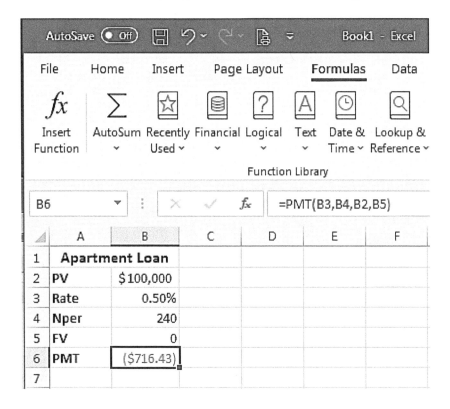

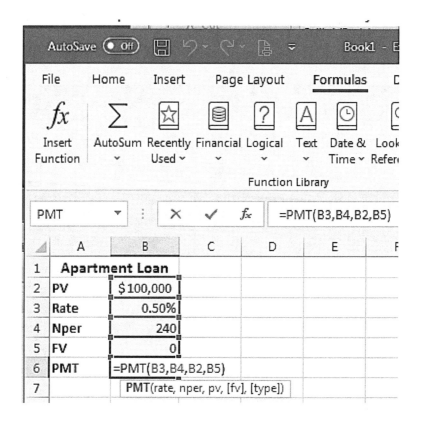

5. The formula allows you to examine the change in the monthly payment required to pay off the loan when you alter the rate, present value, or nper.

Number Of Periods (NPER)

The duration of each investment or loan. This can be expressed mathematically in Excel as =NPER(rate,pmt,pv,[fv],[type]).

To determine the total number of repayment periods for this loan, follow these steps:

- Put everything into a table.
- Scroll down the Financial button on the Formulas tab until you see NPER as an option.
- A prompt asking for the inputs appears in the dialogue window. Fill in the appropriate cell addresses.

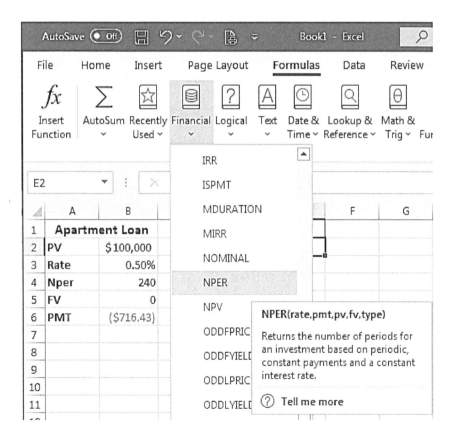

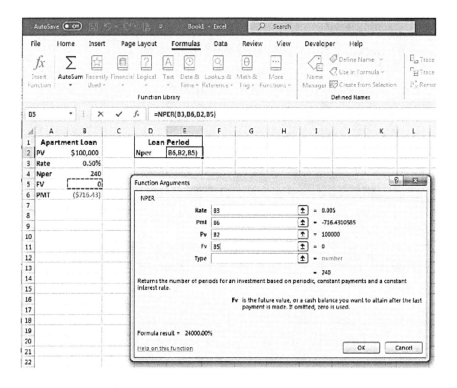

- With twenty years of monthly payments, the Nper lasts for 240 months. In the second screen capture, you can see the NPER formula along with the cells that belong to it. To view the cells that belong to it, double-click on the cell.

- Now that we have the formula, we can see how the number of periods needed to pay off the loan changes as the monthly payment amount changes.

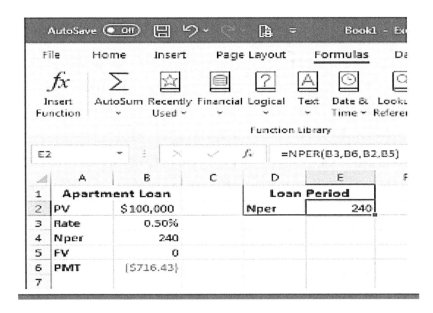

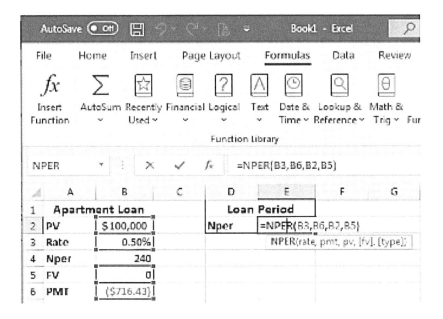

Rate(RATE)

The percentage of investment return needed to earn a predetermined amount over a given time frame, or the interest rate on a loan. This can be expressed mathematically in Excel as =RATE(nper,pmt,pv,[fv],[type],[guess]). It is sufficient to omit the "guess" for our objectives in this case.

To calculate this loan's interest rate, follow these steps:

- ❖ Put everything into a table.
- ❖ Navigating to the Financial button from the Formulas tab In the drop-down menu, locate RATE by scrolling down.
- ❖ You can input the positions of the matching cells in the dialogue window that opens.
- ❖ Rate: half a percent. The second screen capture displays the Rate formula along with the cells that are linked to it. To view the cells that belong to it, double-click on the cell.

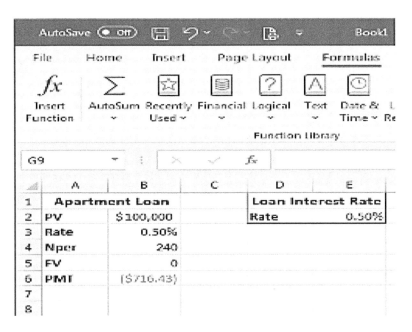

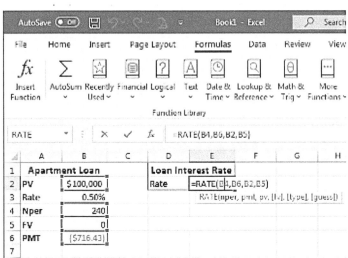

Present Value(Pv)

A loan's or investment's present value, calculated using a constant interest rate, for example a mortgage or loan. I calculated this using the formula =PV(rate,nper,pmt,[fv],[type]) in Excel.

In order to determine the PV for an alternative loan, let's tweak the situation slightly. Find the present value of a loan with the following parameters: interest rate of 6%, term of 20 years, monthly payment of $952.69.

The present value of this loan can be calculated by inserting the same formulas as previously.

E2			X	✓	f_x	=PV(B3,B4,-B6,B5)	
	A	B	C		D	E	
1	Apartment Loan				Present Value		
2	PV				PV	$120,999.66	
3	Rate	0.60%					
4	Nper	240					
5	FV	0					
6	PMT	$952.69					
7							

⊿	A	B	C	D	E	F	G
1	Apartment Loan				Present Value		
2	PV			PV	=PV(B3,B4,B6,B5)		
3	Rate	0.60%			PV(rate, nper, pmt, [fv], [type])		
4	Nper	240					
5	FV	0					
6	PMT	$952.69					
7							

Based on the amounts entered for the previous case, the present value of this loan is $120,999.66, or $121,000 rounded up.

Future Value(FV)

What an investment could be worth in the future if interest rates remain constant and payments are made at regular intervals. This can be expressed mathematically in Excel as =FV(rate,nper,pmt,[pv],[type]).

To find the FV for a different loan's term, let's switch up the circumstance once more. Is it possible to pay off a loan with a 20-year term and 5% interest at the end of that time? If so, how much would the remaining balance be?

To find this out, just use the FV function in the same way as before when inserting the formulas.

O2   ▼ ⋮   ✕ ✓ f_x =FV(L3,L4,L6,L2)

	K	L	M	N	O
1	**Apartment Loan**			**Future Value**	
2	PV	$ 125,000		FV	($0.00)
3	Rate	0.50%			
4	Nper	240			
5	FV	0			
6	PMT	($895.54)			
7					

PMT   ▼ ⋮   ✕ ✓ f_x =FV(L3,L4,L6,L2)

	K	L	M	N	O	P	Q
1	**Apartment Loan**			**Future Value**			
2	PV	$ 125,000		FV	=FV(L3,L4,L6,L2)		
3	Rate	0.50%			FV(rate, nper, pmt, [pv], [type])		
4	Nper	240					
5	FV	0					
6	PMT	($895.54)					
7							

Yes, at the end of the specified time period, the loan's future value will be zero.

TIPS AND TRICKS

1. Use the Format Painter

The "format painter" tool in Excel makes it easy to rapidly format several cells with a single or multiple formats. This comes in handy when you wish to highlight and color-code specific cells. Pick out the cell whose formatting you wish to replicate, then go to the main menu and choose "Format Painter." After that, just choose the cell that you wish to insert the formatting into. When you double-click the icon for several cells, it will remain active until you choose to deselect it.

2. Select The Whole Spreadsheet

You might have to change a whole spreadsheet if you have to. Pressing "Ctrl" and "A" simultaneously will select all cells. Instead of painstakingly scrolling through the spreadsheet with your computer's mouse, this lets you choose the entire thing.

3. Import Data

Importing data instead of copying and pasting might be the way to go when dealing with complicated sets of information. To accomplish this with Excel, go to the "Data" tab and then choose the option to import external data. After you've located your external source, you may import its data into your sheet by following the on-screen directions.

4. Copy And Paste In Multiple Cells

If you wish to duplicate data in many cells, you may do it by selecting the cells you wish to duplicate from and then pasting the information into the last cell you choose. To copy and paste the data from the final cell, press the "Ctrl" and "Enter" keys. Afterwards, it will fill up all the cells that you chose.

5. See Every Formula

Your job may need you to often collaborate with coworkers by sharing spreadsheets. You may find the formulas used by the creator of a spreadsheet by going to the "Formulas" tab. After that, to see the formulas that other people have used, click the "Show formulas" button.

6. Freeze rows and columns

The more data you enter into some spreadsheets, the more difficult they may become to use. Freezing specific rows and columns in your spreadsheet can help you discover what you need faster. To freeze a certain row or column in an Excel spreadsheet, first find it. The next step is to open the "View" menu and then choose "freeze panes" from the submenu.

7. Repeat Designs

Put the initial few digits of a pattern into the right row or column of cells in Excel if you want it to copy the pattern fast. Then, in the final cell on the right-hand side, click the little square. Use the dragging square to choose which cells to copy the pattern to. When you open Excel, the cells will be filled with the right figure.

8. Keep Columns And Rows Hidden

To make more room in a spreadsheet, you can hide columns that aren't being used at the moment. To hide rows or columns, just click the "format" button on the home menu after selecting the row or column header you want to freeze. Select "hide columns" after you've chosen "hide & unhide" or "hide columns."

9. Cut, Paste, And Drag And Drop Spreadsheets

Copies of data or calculations may need to be made across other spreadsheets if your job description calls for it. Simply open both spreadsheets, click on the tab of the one you wish to copy the information from, and then press "Ctrl" to copy. Press "F2" and then "Enter" to continue.

10. Oversee The Use Of Line Breaks

In Excel, you can enter both numbers and letters, but when you write a phrase, sentence, or simply a word, it will go beyond the cell's space. One way to avoid this is to use line breaks and text wrapping to make your work simpler to read. To begin wrapping text, find the cell containing the desired text, go to the "home" tab, and finally, click the "wrap text" button.

11. Make Use Of Copy And Paste

Using the "paste special" option, converting decimals to percentages is a breeze. After you've copied an empty cell and typed "100" into it, you can reformat the cells you've chosen. Hit "paste special" and then choose "divide."

12. Use Flash Fill.

Excel can automatically recreate specific formatting patterns with the help of flash fill. After the second time you enter a pattern, Excel automatically repeats it. For instance, if you want a string of phone numbers to have brackets around the area code and a dash between the third and fourth number, it will be done automatically. If it doesn't work, go to the "data" tab and find the "flash fill" button; that will enable the feature.

13. Divide The Text Into Sections.

Use Excel's "text to columns" function to quickly enter names or other data with several words. If you're pasting a huge dataset but would prefer each word to have its own cell, you can do so by selecting the data. To proceed, go to the "data" tab, then choose "text to columns" and tweak the formatting to your liking.

14. Use A Specialized Paste To Transpose.

You may find yourself in a scenario where you initially intended for specific data to be displayed in rows, but later come to the realization that columns would be more appropriate. Simply copying the desired data allows you to swiftly transpose it from rows to columns or back again. After that, choose "paste special," then press "OK" after checking the "transpose box" option.

15. Add Graphics

If you want to better show off your data in your spreadsheet, you can add images. To accomplish this, choose the cell or element that you would like to display your graphic. Next, right-click and choose "series." The next step is to choose an image or texture fill effect, and then drag and drop the image or graphic you saved into the sheet.

16. Preserve Diagrams For Later Use.

You can use Excel's many graphs and charts, which are fully customizable, to show your data. Unfortunately, your changes won't be saved for when you open a new spreadsheet. By selecting "save as template" from the context menu after you've completed a chart and saving the file as a CRTX, you can create a copy of your customized spreadsheet that you can use for future reference.

17. Control Cells Over Numerous Sheets

A formula exists to help you find data rapidly in a spreadsheet when you have many sheets from which you need to extract it. For everything to function as it should, double-check that the correct data is entered into the same cell on every page of each worksheet. Make a new worksheet and start over. Put the necessary formula into the cell where you'd like to see the result. For instance, if you wish to combine data from different worksheets into one, you can use the formula to copy the contents of the selected cell to the other worksheet you chose.

Add up all the numbers in each cell in the given worksheet, separated by spaces.

18. Keep The Worksheet Hidden

There can be a lot of worksheets inside the spreadsheet you're using. For better organization, you may hide unused worksheets by right-clicking their tab and choosing "hide." This will make it easier to move around the spreadsheet. To reveal the sheet(s) again, choose "unhide" from the "view" choice on the main menu, and then choose the desired sheet(s).

19.Make Use Of Pivot Tables

With pivot tables, you may examine and understand subsets of a massive dataset. Pick out all the rows and columns you'd like the pivot table to look at before you create it. After that, choose "pivot table" from the "insert" tab. After making the necessary adjustments to your table, you may begin to explore your data for trends and patterns.

20. Apply Conditional Formatting To Data
    Visualization

You may make specific values stand out or make
cells easier to find with conditional formatting,
which makes data visualization a breeze. If you want
to make it easier to see the top numbers on a chart,
you can use it to color-code them. From the main
menu, choose the "conditional formatting" icon.
Then, customize the settings to your liking.

21. Create A Menu With A Drop-Down
    Option.

One way to save time in spreadsheets is to establish
a drop-down menu that can be used to populate
certain rows or columns. After you've highlighted
the cell, row, or column you wish to use as a drop-
down menu, go to the "data" tab and then click on
"data validation." After that, select "list" from the
"allow" menu, and then enter your list item
selections under "source."

22. Submit A Picture

If you want to insert a screenshot into your
spreadsheet, just go to the "insert" menu and choose
"screenshot." After that, choose the picture you wish

to insert. Once you've added your image, you can easily format it in your spreadsheet.

23. Halt The Movement Of Cells

Instead of using the original cell as a reference point, the new cell becomes the reference point when you copy and paste a formula into your spreadsheet from another source. By appending a "$" sign preceding the data you wish to retain in the original cell, you can stop the reference from moving to another cell. After that, you can simply cut and paste it.

24. Take Advantage Of Shortcut Keys

When working with spreadsheets, you can save time by using some of Excel's built-in shortcuts. The "Ctrl" key plus a numerical code is the default for most of these shortcuts. To conceal an entire row, for instance, choose it and then hit the "Ctrl" and "9" keys at the same time.

25. Accumulate Without Resorting To Math

Without entering a sum formula, you can easily view the total of a range of cells. Press and hold the "Ctrl" key while you choose the first cell to add, and then do the same with any subsequent cells you wish to combine. To find the sum of those cells, look at the status bar at the bottom of the screen.

26. Emphasize Values That Are Same

Highlighting duplicate values in your sheet can be helpful when dealing with large amounts of data. Select the range of values you wish to highlight, then go to the "styles" page on the home tab, and finally, choose the "highlight cells rule" option. After that, choose the "duplicate values" feature.

www.ingramcontent.com/pod-product-compliance
Lightning Source LLC
LaVergne TN
LVHW051331050326
832903LV00031B/3468